A 4-WEEK COURSE TO LOVE THE LIFE YOU HAVE RIGHT NOW

Feel Better, NO MATTER WHAT

MICHAEL JAMES

This edition first published in the UK and USA in 2021 by
Watkins, an imprint of Watkins Media Limited
Unit 11, Shepperton House
89-93 Shepperton Road
London
N1 3DF

enquiries@watkinspublishing.com

1 3 5 7 9 10 8 6 4 2

Typeset by Lapiz

Printed and bound in the United Kingdom by TJ Books Ltd.

A CIP record for this book is available from the British Library

ISBN: 978-1-78678-417-9 (Paperback)
ISBN: 978-1-78678-467-4 (eBook)

www.watkinspublishing.com

Publisher's note: The information in this book is not intended as a substitute for professional medical advice and treatment. If you are pregnant or are suffering from any medical conditions or health problems, it is recommended that you consult a medical professional before following any of the advice or practice suggested in this book. Watkins Media Limited, or any other persons who have been involved in working on this publication, cannot accept responsibility for any injuries or damage incurred as a result of following the information, exercises or therapeutic techniques contained in this book.

CONTENTS

PREFACE

Recent events had plunged me into an emotional nightmare. My self-esteem was at an all-time low; I felt worthless and unattractive. I couldn't focus on my job. I couldn't do anything. But here I was in the office, having dragged my body to my desk, to spend another day in a job that left me drained and uninspired. I just wanted to disappear.

A colleague came over to speak to me and within moments started pouring out her problems. I didn't particularly mind, but as I tried to focus on the words, my mind pulled away into a storm of my own thoughts. I was drowning. I needed a life raft. I weighed up whether to call the crisis hotline again – or just collapse on the floor. I was in the midst of a panic attack – frozen in the intense pain of overthinking and a whirlwind of emotions…

"You're so laid back," the woman said. "I wish I could be as calm as you."

It is incredible how we can go through these types of battles, in plain view of other people, without it actually being seen. I was startled that she couldn't see what I was experiencing and actually saw the complete opposite – but I couldn't stay with the thought as the self-blame, self-criticism and fear overwhelmed me. I had read all the "must-read" self-help and personal development books out there – but nothing seemed to be working. *What's wrong with me?*, I thought. *Why can't I "be positive", "love myself" or "live in the NOW"?* – whatever that means. *Why can't I "attract" a better life?*

I don't know how I soothed myself that day, but I got through it – only to return to my personal hell a few hours later. I couldn't stop those emotional nightmare storms from coming.

That was then…

INTRODUCTION

EMOTIONAL FREEDOM TO BE YOU

Whether it is in books, on social media or TV, there is a lot of talk these days about self-development and self-empowerment. That, and it seems as though we are endlessly being told to relax, detach from drama, let go, walk away, be positive, live in the moment. Things you have probably heard a hundred or more times but really seem to come down to one thing – fight and change everything you don't like about yourself. I believe this approach amounts to resistance and what we resist persists – but more on that later…

What if I told you that you are *already* a lot more developed than you know and don't need any self-improvement? In fact, what I've found through personal experience, research and my work as a "life coach" is this: each of us, including you, is *already* empowered, and it is this state that I call the *Real Self* – it's the real authentic Self free from the clouds of overthinking; it is who we are.

I started off by looking into different philosophies. I was looking for peace of mind in my own life, so I studied this subject like a PhD, on a quest to find out what really worked. In the books, I found a lot of new, optimistic-sounding ideas, but I still struggled in real life, especially in those times when

I needed it – when I was caught up in overthinking and the emotional challenges of day-to-day living. And, after starting a study group to search for something that *did* work, I realized nothing much was working for anyone else either, it wasn't just me.

Many people explained how they just couldn't get to grips with those so-called easy steps to create a better life they were reading about. They were still battling their emotions and sometimes even felt worse after reading books that demanded positivity at all times. Having to choose the right thoughts to think and be happy all the time was exhausting. And despite reading about the teachings of the latest "enlightened" guru (and even going to events where they could sit in this person's presence for hours), their own lives didn't change much at all.

Others described attending meditation retreats to work on "raising their vibration", or the more impatient would opt for one of those superpowered workshops to learn how to get everything you wanted in a weekend. By Wednesday the following week, after a hyped-up 48 hours, they crashed back to old habits and disappointment. Or months after trying to attract a soulmate or career or life purpose – still nothing.

Many of the popular self-development teachings suggest that some significant change will arrive sometime in the future but before long many people report returning to the same old relationship problems, mood swings and self-worth issues, and more defeated than ever before.

Rituals, breathing techniques, energy practices, movement: the list of "stuff to do" keeps getting longer. It would take a lifetime just to sift through all the available theories, let alone try them. I remember thinking, does living a good life really have to be so complicated?

However, it wasn't all a waste of time. Some aspects of the self-help teachings we explored in the group were soothing and seemed to offer hope. Despite coming from a range of traditions and times in history, these particular aspects shared a universal message: treat others as you want to be treated; be in the present moment; speak your truth – be your authentic self; forgive everyone; love others (and remember you are a person too, so start with loving the person who you are); God is love and love is the real reality – to name but a few. There were so many exciting ideas out there, but the question remained: How do we make these big ideas work in our own everyday lives? No matter how good these concepts sounded, putting them into practice was another thing entirely.

Over the next decade of running my regular group in central London, more insights emerged, and I developed my own system of practical coaching tools, which I then taught to my groups. The results were compelling, tangible and profound, leading to a sustained change for the better in people's lives. My group participants, who came from all backgrounds, told me that the tools were working for them and the changes they were experiencing were sustainable – no matter what was going on. Over the years, these practical teaching tools evolved into a course of coaching tools, which I will be sharing for the first time in this book. Using the tools, I know that you too can feel better no matter what the circumstances you are currently facing or changes you want to make.

In developing the four-week course for this book, I didn't have a magical awakening, and I don't possess any special powers. I simply found a simple, practical approach, which will teach you how to tune in to *your own* inner voice, Real Self or Higher Power (in whatever way you relate to it). In the course, we will be delving into all those everyday situations that life throws at us – romantic relationships, body image concerns, relationships with family, health and healing – and discovering how to find emotional freedom within all of them.

So, this book is a collection of my work, and its purpose is to show you that there is another way to self-acceptance and finding the confidence to live your best life – and you don't need to change

It is about finding emotional freedom wherever you are. It is about loving who you are.

at all. That you are enough, right here and right now – no matter how you may be feeling in the moment. And realizing that you always have been enough – while it is perfectly fine to not see that sometimes. Imagine it as sweeping away whatever may be getting in the way of who you are and clearing your vision until you can see the best in yourself and in life. How to sweep away the clouds that are stopping the light from pouring through.

Freedom to Be You Just as You Are

Everyone wants to feel free to be themselves, free of self-doubt and self-criticism because we know life works out better that way. In following my four-week course, you will come to understand that all your emotional reactions – all those faults and flaws – can be gifts of transformation. You will see how you can be free to accept all your triumphs as well as those times you stumble. How to find freedom from the limitations of the overthinking mind. The mind that tells you "you can't do it" or warns you that "they might judge you if you do". We all have this same mind, and it's your friend when you know how to work with it. And it's the biggest obstacle when you don't.

You might think if you are simply free to be you, then it also means having to put up with any self-limiting behaviours and habits. Or if you are kind and gentle with yourself, you will somehow revert to being a bad person – whatever that means. This seems to be the part of our human nature – deep down, we believe we need to be controlled. This idea may come from our culture, our upbringing, our schooling or some other source, but it doesn't come from spirituality – which tells us we were created in the image of perfection. I believe deep down, we are all perfect, loving, confident, and from this place, we all coexist perfectly together in our differences and diversity.

> You don't need the rules you think you do.

Everything and everyone thrives when they are accepted and treated with love, just as they are. The individual, and the world, come into balance. We are by our nature enlightened, perfect in innocence and goodness – like infants. As we grow up, thoughts – in the form of beliefs, attitude and opinions – all seek to tell us that we are not enough as we are, so we try to cover up or suppress our authentic Selves. But this layer is not us; it is merely covering our true natures which remain, fully formed and perfect.

And that's why you don't need to be fixed. You don't need to heal yourself or work on yourself relentlessly. If you really were created perfect, why would you need to do this? Recall those mentors or teachers who made a difference in your life. These were the ones who saw you – the light or truth in you. They saw who you really are. They didn't offer to fix or change you; they just saw the truth in you. And I hope by reading this book that you know the truth in you, too.

How to Use This Book

I hope by now, you have a sense of the journey on which you are about to embark and how the four-week course is all about *feeling* better rather than *being* better. Through this book, you'll learn to shift gears and appreciate the very thing you thought was a problem and see how your freedom, right here and now, is waiting to be discovered.

Before we start working on the course, we'll explore some principles, which I hope will give you a fresh way of looking at the life stages that we all go through regardless of background, from birth to adulthood – and how this new perspective relates to your own life. You will understand how life is on your side and how self-acceptance and self-love is the key to thriving. You will learn the theory you'll need to put the practical tools which follow into action.

The course starts by helping you to create a solid foundation. You'll get real about exactly where you are and then learn how to clear your mind and detach from your thoughts through meditation. You'll then be ready to trust that you are enough and that everything about you is OK – even the things you may have thought were a problem.

The techniques and tools you'll learn will anchor all these good feelings in your mind, so you can begin to live your best life – confident, connected and appreciating the moment while excited about what's coming. This isn't so much a prescriptive course where you have to do certain things on certain days, but I do share the tools in a specific order, and then it's over to you to try them out. Each practice builds on the one before to bring about lasting, sustainable change. Amazing things happen when you know how to simply be yourself and accept yourself, shining bright as who you are – and this book will show you how.

Then in Part III, we'll explore some of the more challenging aspects of life: body image, romantic and other relationships, for example, and I'll show you how to apply some of the tools you've learned in the course in specific situations. Plus, I'll share some powerful insights direct from my coaching experience.

PART I

HOW LIFE WORKS

CHAPTER 1

EVOLUTION: THE JOURNEY OF BEING HUMAN

Without tension, there is no evolution.

When an organism encounters resistance or challenges, evolution happens. This process occurs without thought or attention – and is common down to the cellular level in all living things in the known universe. The immune system, for example, requires invaders to learn how to fight off attackers and become stronger; it's how it shifts to the next level. Whether it's the white blood cells in your immune system or the entire organism and everything in between, the resistance or challenges become ingredients which benefit future adaptations. The environment and the journey of life itself provides a program of resistance training for the organism to co-create its evolution as it progresses, where it becomes more adapted to live its optimum life. Adversaries can be seen as opportunities to use as resistance in which to evolve. And so, the choice is either taking on challenges, which leads to adapting and thriving, or the species ends. In this way, you can see that curveballs are a bonus, even essential, from the perspective of evolution.

It is the same with human evolution. But we have something different: *thinking*. Our resistance to our thoughts, our mind chatter, is often more challenging than the problems themselves. It is this facet of the human species which makes us unique and separate. Humankind resists more than any other being, and this is why our evolution has outstripped all others. We receive the gains of our development faster too, within our lifetime, rather than waiting for future generations alone to experience these "upgrades".

One way of looking at life is that you are here for this evolution – and for the interest and enjoyment of the experience. For many people, life is a struggle to get somewhere else all the time; they are fixated on the problems – the weightlifting itself rather than the gains that can come from it. What stands between you and your Real Self is what are sometimes called "blocks" or "patterns", which are often things like insecurity, shame, guilt, fear, self-criticism and even self-hatred. You are already your Real Self. But how do you get there? How do you realize this for yourself?

Stage 1: Born as Your Perfect, Free Self

You were born perfect, enlightened – your real, authentic Self like a mini sun radiating knowing. You can see this aura, this glow, this joy in very young children, as they seem to outshine everyone around them. They are not experts at personal development or positive thinking, and they don't need to be. Instead, life simply works for them: they are loveable and fun to be around; they manifest better than most adults (look at them get the lion's share of presents on birthdays and holidays – and almost everyone loves them). Someone said, "Become as little children", and this might be what they meant. It is about coming from your natural, innocent, Real Self mindset. And this is the same for all of us – how we all begin. We didn't think much, we just followed our flow, our instincts and our intuition.

The Real Self is that part of you that always exists, no matter what your current mood may be. Like the sun, your Real Self can't be extinguished and continues to shine, no matter how many clouds (our mind chatter) get in the way. It is thinking which stops us from remembering that we are, and always have been, free, ever powerful, always confident – and have the capacity to evolve to be more so. And your Real Self is dominant when you are in flow, in the zone, and synced up or centred in who you are.

Being your Real Self means being yourself, free from the clutter of thoughts.

Stage 2: Moving into Adulthood

In this next stage, it may feel like you have lost your childhood innocence. Except that's not possible, because while you may have fallen asleep, your Real Self remains intact, untouched, no matter what your experiences. For some, this stage of life is dramatic, and for others, not so much. For others still, the events might not be so traumatic, but their *reactions* to what happens are. To use a gym metaphor, *this is your workout.*

The intellect or mind chatter is necessary if we want to evolve – but so often it is a terrible guide and confuses us. But this confusion, too, is part of the design of life. So, while you might feel like you are lost, you are actually evolving. Everyone feels this tension at some time or another – it is due to thinking and your resistance to thinking; *it means you have gone into your thoughts.*

When you get involved with the thinking mind, you apply resistance to your life experience. Some people call this "negative thinking", but this label is part of the problem. You don't call the resistance at the gym "negative" (although it doesn't always feel easy) because you understand it is *beneficial.* In fact, most of us *choose* this resistance and *pay money* to experience it. Yet with life, it's a different story. We are told tension is never good for us. And this approach isn't working.

The tension of life evolves your skills, your power and your self-worth. It creates your best life. It brings out the best version of you. So, take something like *insecurity*, for example, it is to be thanked, as it is the workout for *confidence. Self-hate*, even, is a workout: *it's a workout for self-confidence or self-love.* There is nothing wrong with feeling all kinds of emotions and having all kinds of thoughts – no matter what you may have been told. Thoughts, both "positive" and "negative", are the workout that evolves your life and that is their benefit.

So, there is nothing wrong with experiencing tension or mind chatter. Like the exercise equipment at the gym, the mind provides the tension and resistance you need to evolve. This is the journey to create self-empowerment. Nothing has gone wrong. You are OK where you are. A perception of powerlessness is the weightlifting to your self-empowerment. Like all evolution, it is the challenges which evolve the strengths.

No thoughts, no problems: it is your own thoughts that are in your way. And yet, this tension is your friend because it contributes to the evolution of life.

Stage 3: Returning to Your Real Self Mindset

Now you come back. You return to innocence. You return to the connection with your Real Self and can see the mind chatter for what it is. You wake up and become "as a child" again. But it is better now, thanks to your coming off track and you have evolved hugely. It's an exciting process and what the four weeks of this course will help you receive the benefits of in your own life.

Going through this process, adapting and thriving in response to change, life continues to get better. Of course, it may not feel that way at the time. But just as if you were to focus only on the weights at the gym, you'd miss noticing how your body was changing. What's more, if you lifted weights without any rest, then the gains wouldn't happen. And if you didn't lift at all, you wouldn't gain muscle. So, tension and relaxation are both necessary. And so, it is about going

> Being your Real Self is the key to accessing your evolutionary gains sooner rather than later – those gains that are here now. It is like opening the door and letting them in.

into thinking – and then stepping back from thinking. This is the way to evolution – and to receive the gains of this evolution.

Realizing Real Self – Being Yourself

In my own life, I went into overthinking, depression and anxiety. Life became frightening and unpleasant. Little did I know this was my evolution. Because when you are battling your evolution, it's hard to see the benefits. Of course, it is frightening, and it seems pointless and unkind when you don't know the full story. Seeing it this way, the planet is like a gym for the powerful beings that we are. Life is about enjoying the evolutionary experience. It is about the freedom to express yourself fully. It is about feeling how you feel and not worrying about it – that same freedom you had as a child.

In some philosophical teachings or societies, diversity is discouraged. Those with strong reasons for being and new ideas are ostracized. And yet, we are here to express who we are. It is only the limited human thought mechanism or mind chatter, that would ever want to repress who we are. But this repression too is part of the journey, and it is yet more resistance training.

> It is all good: repression is the "weight" that creates more freedom.

Many people settle for following the crowd, social norms and what is in or out, due to the fear of not fitting in. It takes courage to live as your Real Self. But those characters who are themselves, despite sometimes being frowned upon, emerge as the legendary lights history remembers – while also living their best lives.

CHAPTER 2
LIFE IS A MIRROR

Life reflects back what you feel about you.

When you feel that amazing, in-the-zone feeling – like you are *it* – you don't need the world's approval. You don't need anything at all. And in this state of completion, you are given the world. You feel clear-minded and confident in a particular area of life, and it usually works out. This is because life reflects back our level of confidence and self-value. As a result, life itself becomes a teacher of self-empowerment. In this way, confidence is indeed everything – the rest is commentary.

Because here's the thing: you are already "it". Life isn't about becoming more or better but about *realizing* the truth of who you already are. Some of the most significant spiritual texts tell us we are made in a divine image. But if you don't realize this right now, this is good too, because every time you feel less than great, it's evolution in action.

All too often, we look to others for love and acceptance before we love or accept ourselves. As we move into the second stage, into adulthood and overthinking ("weight training"), we begin to look for someone to tell us we are amazing: to be "discovered" or "special", for example. This approval-seeking starts in childhood as we seek to make our parents or caregivers happy with us. The trouble is that even if we do find outside approval, it will never be enough. Instead, we just search for more and more, not knowing that it is *self*-confidence and *self*-love we are really looking for. Life, therefore, simply mirrors back our current level of self-love and acceptance of ourselves. We don't get what we want so much as what we *already know we are.*

> When you clear the mirror by clearing your thoughts, your true beauty is reflected back.

All that really matters is your opinion of you – not what other people say about you or what's going on in your life right now. What matters is what *you* feel about you, and then life will reflect that right back at you. This isn't a reward or punishment but a tool you can use to develop more self-confidence and embody the incredible person that you are, right here and now.

> Most of us are longing for that wholeness within – that sense of Self. Someone who is self-contained and fulfilled is at their most attractive and compelling.

I'm sure this isn't the first time you've heard about the importance of self-worth. The question is: *How* do I feel self-confident? *How* do I love myself? And that is where the four-week course comes in.

Why It's OK to Be You and to Feel How You Feel

Princes and princesses don't feel like princes and princesses all the time – and that's OK. *Everyone* has inner battles and storms. We hide this inner life, however, because we don't feel like it is attractive. Would you post an unflattering photo of yourself on Instagram after a hard workout looking exhausted? Probably not. That's not being inauthentic – it's understandable. But it means everyone is hiding parts of themselves, making you feel like you're the only one with this internal workout, while everyone else is walking around being perfect all of the time – with no other emotions.

The goal of feeling confident *all the time* seems as though it is a good idea, but it's both impractical and virtually impossible. So many people force themselves to be positive, no matter where they are and what's going on. Of course, this attitude arises from having good intentions. But there is also a time for our training, and you want to allow that. This is also why so many of the positive-thinking teachings can actually teach us to beat up on ourselves. Loving yourself is loving *all* parts of yourself: the times you are in the zone and the times when you are not – when you are working out.

You wouldn't be mad at a champion athlete for feeling exhausted during training. You would know that this was part of their preparation. Later on, when they are on the track, they can shine and be amazing and feel in the zone. But their training time is not about the star performance, it's about the training.

Resistance to the way you feel is the problem – not the way you feel.

Let's face it, we all feel all kinds of emotions. No one I've met stays in an exact steady, unchanging state of joy or happiness or confidence. And what if that's how it's meant to be? What if *all* emotions are good?

The problem isn't that you feel needy or desperate, for example, because everyone feels that way sometimes. It is not the feeling that's unattractive or off-putting – but the lack of self-acceptance. It is that you're not accepting yourself, this mood or feeling. You are not embracing that feeling, which you might call "neediness", as the weightlift you require right now to get the muscle you want. Everyone feels neediness sometimes, and in fact, another definition of neediness is "ambition", which is necessary for creating big dreams. Ambition can sometimes feel uncomfortable and implies discontentment, but it's not seen as a feeling to be ashamed of. It is this shift in perspective that can help you accept your feelings. Because if you could allow your feelings to be, you would get out of your own way and find freedom.

Thinking Mind vs Real Self

Most people's approach is to think thoughts throughout their day – whatever mind chatter comes into their mind – but this activity is the cause of most of our, and the world's, misery. Forget what you've read about the power of thoughts: thinking will get you nowhere as far as answers go and I call this our "lower-self" mindset.

I'm not saying the thinking mind is always the bad guy, but thoughts tend to provide tension, not answers. The mind chatter works out our muscles and our best life. Yes, our thoughts produce resistance, but it's only a machine for us to use. We don't have to be part of the mechanics; we can step aside and into our Real Self, which communicates not through thought but insights, knowledge, intuition and instinct.

The problem is that we have been brought up to think we *are* the thinking mind, that it's our guide and to listen to its advice – even though it is pretty much always wrong. Because we haven't been told that there's another way, we continue overthinking, and criticizing ourselves for overthinking, and life gets worse. We don't realize there is another guide that we can tune to. When you are your Real Self, you are not aware of your mind chatter at all. You are an open channel to insights, knowledge, intuition and ideas; you know what to do, and you feel like you are incredible – which you are.

So, the battle within is between the intellect and intuition: the lower-self mind vs the inner or Real Self. The lower-self's intellect is limited and tiny as a source of wisdom; the Real Self is limitless. But the lower-self mind chatter is often louder and initially more appealing to us than the Real Self. By taking part in the four-week course, you will experience the clarity and certainty of your Real Self coming to the fore, while the "static in the radio" confusion of the lower-self mind chatter will quiet and step down.

CHAPTER 3

UNCONDITIONAL SELF-ACCEPTANCE

Just love yourself more.

I had just finished teaching at my group in London when a few of the regulars started discussing how much they were enjoying it, and how it was like nothing else they'd found. At the end of these evenings, I would always feel amazing too. Still, on this particular occasion, this group had flooded me with so many compliments and were so full of gratitude that it uplifted the vibe to another level. They began offering suggestions about how I could share my message through marketing, doing more classes and workshops, an audiobook, online events and so on. They enthusiastically suggested all these good ideas – all great ideas. Then, one woman, who hadn't offered any suggestions, interrupted the group and turned to me: "No, no, no, you don't need to do anything. You just need to do one thing. You need to love yourself more," she smiled. "Just like you tell us to."

Rather than feel judged or exposed, this woman's clarity landed powerfully, and I paused, feeling the impulse to really listen to what she was saying. She paused, too – and that was the message in its entirety. The answer was to love myself more. *And only that.*

At that time, this message of unconditional self-acceptance and being gentle with yourself as a practical route to empowerment was a new one that I'd been sharing. I had been teaching how our number-one block is endlessly self-criticizing. Now, I was being called to put this into practice: to appreciate myself and be gentle with myself at a deeper level; to accept myself more deeply than I had before.

Getting Out of Your Own Way

Like so many of us, I was used to being harsh with myself. The positive side of this, like a strict and self-disciplined athlete, is that my inner critic has pushed me on to go deeper and deeper into questions to discover the answers I needed. But like any habit, abusing the self becomes automatic, and we can become accustomed to telling ourselves things that don't honour us. Even though I had made huge shifts in my life, there was still more work to be done, and areas in which I wasn't fully embracing who I was. Discovering new areas and understanding that it is an ongoing journey is great news: knowing how much better life can get, when it is already fairly good.

When you are self-accepting and gentle with yourself – even for being self-critical – this allows your false, overthinking self to step aside and your natural power to step forward. Although the evolutionary journey of harshness is perfectly OK, gentleness is the way and so you want to be gentle with your harsh side, too. Just realize you are doing the best you can in every moment. Being gentle with *all* aspects of yourself. This is true self-love.

Some believe it is narcissistic to love yourself as a priority. But narcissism is the opposite of self-love and inner confidence. Narcissism is the constant craving of love from others and neediness for attention from the world – often resorting to manipulation to get it. Narcissism only ever leads to an empty existence and comes from a total *lack* of self-worth. When you feel good about yourself, when you practise love for self, you won't crave or need anything from out there. And that, in fact, is often the moment you get everything from "out there".

Practise Unconditional Self-acceptance

Remind yourself to practise self-acceptance by being gentle with yourself no matter what. This doesn't mean feeling good all the time – it means accepting yourself as you are and your life as it is, even in those moments you think you can't. When you are self-accepting of all parts of yourself, when you realize it's OK to be you, life flows more smoothly. And the process takes less time than you might think. So how does it work?

Being fully yourself feels authentic, so you'll find it easier to express yourself freely and honestly. Because you are free to experience all your emotions, you don't hold yourself to the impossible task of being perfectly happy all the time. Doing this, you will quickly realize those parts of you that you once thought were ruining your life are actually your greatest gifts. As you honour yourself more, you'll feel more confidence and life will mirror back this feeling of self-confidence. So, you respect and appreciate yourself more and life respects and appreciates you right back.

When you start being gentle with all aspects of yourself and self-accepting of all your facets and emotions, you'll probably stumble a few times. All this is training. All this is evolving your success. All this is part of the journey – and it's all OK. As you read these words, you may want to feel your breath and let your breath guide you. Take a deep breath in… and breathe out. Right here and right now, you are perfect, and you are loved. You are on track. There is nowhere to get to. This is the ideal place to begin. There is nothing to search for in the static of thoughts – the answers you seek are much closer than that.

In any moment, you are either thinking, or you are loving. You can't think and love at the same time. Analysis, justifying, debating, trying to prove a point – it is all thinking. And that is OK. You are evolving yourself (thinking), or you're being more fully yourself (centred in your Real Self) – and both are OK. You are either in relaxed confidence mode allowing your gains – or you are in workout mode, creating gains. It's win-win.

Where you are is OK. The solution to whatever you are dealing with now is to love yourself more. Love is the doorway to the Real Self, which has the answers to everything.

Unconditional Self-acceptance is the Way to Change

Self-empowerment and freedom begin with realizing you can feel fearful and guilty and anxious and be OK with that. You can feel your feelings just as they are, and you can accept each and every one. You can embrace them all. Rather than comparing your life to some ideal of how it should be, realize your life is your life.

We all start from different places. It isn't a competition to get anywhere the fastest. If you had a poverty-stricken childhood, it's not reasonable to expect to feel wealthy immediately. If you have been brought up to self-hate, how can you expect to have perfectly healthy relationships right now? You are doing the best you can – and self-acceptance starts with realizing that anyone in your position would react how you are reacting right now. It's OK to have your beliefs. It's OK to have your reactions to life. It's OK to be you, just as you are, right now. Relentlessly trying to change or improve yourself is self-criticism and counterproductive; it keeps you stuck.

Sometimes when people try to fix us or offer a suggestion when we haven't asked them – it makes us feel as though we're not doing it right or we can't do it by ourselves. The words are well-intentioned, but it just doesn't work. You want to instead begin by reassuring yourself that right here and right now you are doing OK. Because you are. So, when you're unsure, ask yourself, "Am I loving and being myself – or trying to improve myself?"

So now you know the real story: you are already personally developed. Your job is to look deeper and *reveal* your ideal life more than it is to create anything or radically change anything. And that is what we are going to focus on in the following course.

The best personal development begins by realizing that we are already personally developed.

PART II

FEEL BETTER, NO MATTER WHAT: A FOUR-WEEK COURSE

HOW TO USE THE FOUR-WEEK COURSE

The essence of the course: clear your mind and be You.

Now you understand the foundations of the training, let's make a start on the course. There are four sessions over the four weeks, with work to do in between. Four weeks to consistently feel better. Are you ready?

Week 1

Bring to mind where you are and what's going on for you at this time. Imagine a road. Sometimes, it is like we are in the stationary traffic of overthinking at this point, without much power and knowledge of what to do. This is the mental plane. It is noisy, so much chatter, and like a treadmill, getting nowhere. Here we hand over all of your issues with the *Higher Power List,* and then you'll learn to clear your mind (the "traffic jam" of thoughts) through *Focal-point Meditation*, and then learn some useful techniques to deal with stressful or overwhelming emotions when they occur.

Week 2

When you are stuck in slow-moving traffic, you don't have many options. You can either be OK with where you are or get annoyed about it. And so this week, you'll find a way to be OK with where you are with the *"What's Good About…" List* and then the *Freedom Process,* which is a unique way to find emotional freedom by revealing the good in any challenging situation. You'll then move into appreciating all the positives in your life and explore the *Confidence Evoke*, a powerful technique to develop and practise being in a confident state in all areas of your life.

Week 3

This part of the course is all about taking your power back in your relationships and developing self-love and self-acceptance. You'll learn how to "press" the *Magic Button* to instantly regain your power if you've been giving it away. Building on this, you'll get to connect to the person within you, your Real Self, through the gentle yet profound *Self-realization Process.* The *Relationship Trigger* takes this self-love to a deeper level – and is also an absolutely revolutionary way to deal with the pain and disempowerment that can come up in relationships.

Week 4

By this point, you will be clear-minded and feeling good, uplifted to a "superhighway" state of being and ready to learn how to live in that state of confidence. You'll start to feel comfortable residing above the clouds of thought, where you are open to an unrestricted flow of ideas – which is the language of your Real Self. Here, there is no friction, and nothing weighs you down. This is about being free to be yourself in all areas of life. How do you sustain this mood? I share *FreeSelf Anchors (Declarations),* the *Retrospective Process*, and how to create a *Starboard*, to stand in your power then live your life from that empowered state.

> Techniques and tools are marked with 🕊 and are introduced over the four-week course. It's a good idea to find time for at least three practices a day but do what works best

for you. At the end of the course, on page 119, you'll find a chart of all the tools and practices covered, which you can use to create your own personalized daily plan.

Disciplined Practice Brings Freedom

To many people, any kind of regimented routine seems to be going the opposite way to personal freedom. But commitment and follow-through during the course will open your way to freedom from your thoughts. Freedom and discipline also probably sound like opposites according to your mind chatter, which, be warned, is going to resist doing these practices. It's that very mind chatter which tries to talk you out of anything which benefits you (like going to the gym, or meditation, or starting a new hobby or interest that would improve your experience of life). It's that mind chatter that is the primary obstacle to freedom and being your Real Self. These practices work to sweep away mind chatter so you can *feel good now,* but you've got to do them to see the results.

You can see the door but not what's behind it until you've done the practices. The freedom you are seeking is the freedom from that mind chatter.

Starting with Week 1, read through the chapter and give yourself some time to practise the tools each week. If you'd like to fast-track, wait a day or two rather than the suggested week, but make sure that you spend some time to let the ideas sink in. You will learn the techniques in a specific order for a reason, so I suggest following the course in the order it has been written initially, and then – once you're more familiar with the techniques – you can choose the ones which work best for you.

You'll probably find that new ideas will drop into your mind as you work your way through the course because, as you clear the clouds of your thinking, new ideas and intuition will shine through. This is clarity: knowing precisely what to do when and filled with new uplifting ways to look at your current life situations.

Many of the ideas were developed by me, others are my own take on the "classic" and sometimes misinterpreted self-help techniques which so many people have taught over time (such as meditation or writing lists of things you are grateful for). However, all of the practices I share are ways to *feel better no matter what*, from right where you are. This course is less about looking to the future and more about finding a way to shift your perspective *now* to enjoy *now.* And when you do that, you'll discover how life just works out for you.

WEEK 1

BEGINNING: CONNECT, TUNE IN AND FOCUS

Hand over whatever is bothering you and clear your mind.

This week you'll learn how to set your intentions for the course ahead, throwing out all that "clutter" from your mind and handing it over to a Higher Power. Once this is out of the way, I'll teach you a new approach to meditation which I call *Focal-point Meditation*. Use the following week to practice these new techniques daily. Finally, I'll share some of my most effective tools for when you are feeling awful, and nothing else seems to be working: to overcome emotional overwhelm. Rather than daily tools, take these ones out of the bag when you need them – when you're feeling so wound up and upset and out of centre that you want instant soothing. You can have a go with each one and find out which one you prefer and which one works best for you.

We all need to express ourselves and be heard. Although I understand, and teach, that some of this is our stories and interpretations, they still must be acknowledged first. Working one-to-one with people, I find they tend to share whichever area of life they want to. They explain how they are feeling about their romantic or family relationships, things they want to change or improve. Any career challenges, problems with money, body image or health, dreams or ambitions they want to happen. Fears about the world, stress levels, overthinking, anxiety.

If you don't share your stories, this secrecy can give the stories power, and you can get stuck in them. So, explaining what's going on in your life is an essential first step. Although it's probably worth adding that I advise limiting diving into the past too much. You can, of course, return to your past experiences as you go along – but our focus is moving into the clear-minded space of the present moment, rather than being held back by the clutter of past stories.

And so just as though you were in one-to-one coaching with me, this first week is all about explaining where you are and then beginning to clear your mind by handing over your problems and starting a meditation practice. It's about building a foundation and preparing you for the more profound work to come.

Techniques and tools are marked with 🕊 and are introduced over the four-week course. It's a good idea to find time for at least three practices a day but do what works best for you. At the end of the course, on page 119, you'll find a chart of all the tools and practices covered, which you can use to create your own personalized daily plan.

Hand Over Your Problems and Focus on "Your Work"

🕊 *Higher Power List*

At this point, thinking about your problems and what's not working might be making you feel a little overwhelmed, so I'd like you to start by doing this simple process I call the *Higher Power List*, which involves handing these problems to a Higher Power. It is time to "cast your cares", to get all the details and the stories and the dramas out of your mind and hand them over to what you see as your Higher Power.

Get a piece of paper or a notepad and draw a line down the left-hand side of a page to create a margin, and then a line across the top, two inches down, to create a margin across the top. On the top left-hand side corner, in the small space created by the lines, write "Me". On the top right-hand side, you write "Higher Power". You can also write other words on the right-hand side, such as Life, the Universe, Divine Love, Creator or God, in fact, whatever name or word/s feels best to you to describe that power source that flows through you and through everything in life. This list is also known as the *Real Self List* (and I wrote about it in my previous book, *Emotional First Aid – How to Feel Better in Times of Crisis*) – and some people like to write "Real Self" in place of Higher Power.

Higher Power

Now, under the *Higher Power* heading, write down all the things on your mind in the form of requests. For example:

- *Sort out my relationship with Mark.*
- *Centre me in my Real Self.*
- *Show me the next step to take.*
- *Show me the right decision to make.*
- *Show me my life purpose.*

You are "throwing" those requests on to the Higher Power's side. Those issues which you have no answer to right now and are getting in your way. It's almost as if you're saying to life "You sort this out." It's these dilemmas which are blocking the very solutions you are looking for. All this thinking is "snow in the snow globe" blocking your clear vision. Anything on your mind, keep on throwing it onto the right-hand side.

Putting the story on paper can bring clarity to a busy or overwhelmed mind. You throw over all that mind chatter onto the right-hand side. This process clears your mind. It passes over all those things that you've been trying to figure out but can't seem to figure out – because the best use of the mind isn't to solve problems. Thinking gets *in the way* of solutions.

This exercise is about acknowledging that there is something wiser than your thinking mind. There's a Higher Power which can deal with your problems better than your thinking mind, and it's about giving all your issues and overthinking to that part of you. It is not about making a wish list. It's about throwing all those problems and thoughts and wants on to the right-hand side to get them out of your mind so you can enjoy your life from right now, leaving life to sort everything out. It's a practice to clear your mind.

More Examples: *Higher Power List*

Show me the truth about this situation/person: Writing this on the right-hand side is a request to see things differently. To see clearly and from a different angle. If you don't feel good about the situation, you can't see it from an accurate, "higher" perspective. This is also one of the best ways to forgive someone. You are asking for a new perception: the perception that your Real Self sees. A fresh perception might get you to see that nothing went wrong, and everything is OK – and sometimes leads to an instant letting go. You don't have to think about the "hows", just throw it on the right-hand side.
Sort out my relationship: Any relationship which isn't working well, hand it over – and even hand over the ones that *are* working, to take them up a level.
Bring me a dynamic new hobby or interest: I often encourage writing this down. If you don't find an outside interest, your dynamic hobby will tend toward worry and drama because the mind loves to think; it would rather go into fearful things than do nothing. That's why scary movies are so popular – they're exciting to the mind on some level. Engaging with a new project or a hobby pulls us out of the overthinking. However, you need something more dynamic and exciting to the mind than your overthinking. So, remember to add the word *dynamic* to your request. Don't go searching for something exciting; leave it to life to bring you the idea of what it may be. Often, a friend will randomly suggest something, or you will notice something online and feel "that's it!"

One of my coaching clients described to me how she was worried about a relationship, and her main hobby or interest became the relationship. What the other person was doing and so on. She needed a hobby to compete with that one. So, on the right-hand side, she wrote: "Get me excited about my life", "Bring me a passion and a purpose". And it is the same if you are looking for love: you need a hobby bigger than the search for love. The dynamic interest gets your attention off the problem and out of the way up on the superhighway level, opening up a space for new ideas while life can get in there and sort it all out.

Help me "Be More Me": This is another great one to write down. Being yourself is in many ways one of the big secrets of life. Most people are trying to be more like someone else they feel is a "successful person". Doing this, you just see yourself as a second-rate them; you lose your power and might find it hard to get above average. So rather than compete with millions of people all doing the same thing, be yourself, and then you have no competition because no one else can be you. If you bring to mind all the people you rate as successful – be it, superstars in the field of music, movies, sports or business, they would have one thing in common: they are all being themselves more than the competition is being themselves. So, surrender this statement on to the right-hand side as a reminder.

Surround me with support: For some people, this is a request for supportive people to show up in their life. For others, it's about relaxing into the trust of divine beings – like having a spirit guide or guardian angel. It's about just knowing you don't have to do it all yourself and writing this down frees you to get on with the left-hand side of the list – your focusing practices, which we will get to in a minute. Send angels to smooth your day ahead or your destination if you're travelling – if that feels good to you. You can also surround loved ones or friends or anyone on your mind with angels in this way.

Keep thoughts at bay and anchor me in my Real Self: This statement is like putting a doorman at the door of your mind. It keeps you focused and your mind clear.

Further things to cast over to the Higher Power side could be, for example:

- *Sort out all situations and bless them with success.*
- *Show me what to do.*
- *Help me clearly hear my guidance and follow through with it.*
- *Sort out all my friendships – allow only those who love and respect me in my life.*

Choose whatever wording feels best and keep on casting your cares on the right-hand side.

Me

Now move to the left-hand margin – the side with "Me". Here write down all of the techniques you decide to do from this course as well as your existing daily practices. This will be your reminder to do the most important tasks of all – those techniques to clear your mind and allow you to be more you, right here and right now. Once you've done your practices, put a tick next to them.

At this stage in the course, before learning all of the techniques, I recommend adding any of your current mind-clearing practices to the left-hand side. If you are not doing much as yet, leave it blank, to add to your list as you learn them.

Clearing the Mind and Stepping Aside from Thinking

Focal-point Meditation

Next, I want to talk about meditation, which is a vital part of the course, and why it's being introduced in the first week. First, you want to get clear. You want some separation between you and your thinking mind, which you want to put back in its place as a servant, not the master it has been. You may already be meditating regularly, and that's great – and I hope this section will provide further insights and clarification of how to deepen your practice.

When you are busy overthinking, it clouds your confidence. You are not your Real Self. When you step back from your thoughts, the clouds clear, and you become more confident. One definition of confidence could be "the state of not thinking". Confidence is the Real Self – that credible part of you that is always there behind the confusion of mind chatter.

Confidence is your natural state, like the sun always shining behind the clouds of overthinking.

As much as the mind chatter wants you to think – and to rush forward – first allow your thoughts to settle. Picture a snow globe waiting for the snowflakes to settle – with a little patience, the vision becomes clear. This is meditation. Most personal development is about rearranging thoughts, which is like trying to rearrange snowflakes in a snow globe. Things change, but nothing changes. With *Focal-point Meditation*, you allow the thoughts to settle by bringing your attention to something else. It is like opening a channel unclouded by thought. Imagine a clear pipeline swept clear of debris, so the water flows freely. When your thoughts are out of the way, the Real Self's ideas flow. There's none of those opinions or judgements or worries or dramas – just a flow of who you really are, which is all-accepting and allowing of life just as it is. This is the real power everyone is looking for. Meditation integrates you into your Real Self – it sorts everything out. That's because the Real Self doesn't think thoughts: it's the source of ideas behind the snowstorm of thoughts.

Some people argue with me at this point and say, "I don't need to meditate." They want to move on to the "proper exercises". They don't have time to meditate (I hear this even when someone has a lot of spare time). The thing is the foundation of a house must be built before constructing the walls and adding a roof. This stage is crucial.

Some people also think meditation will slow them down; they imagine all these spiritual teachers with lives they can't relate to, just sitting there and talking about being still – and so they associate meditation with a slow, mundane life. This is not true; meditation gets rid of what is in the way of your fun and excitement. It connects you with your passion. It reveals your Real Self. Some people's Real Self – like those teachers that come to mind – may be living differently to how you want to live – living more simply and calmly, while others may be travelling all over the place living busier, more exciting lives. We are all different and meditation will have a different effect depending on who you are – but it always allows the real you to step forward. Meditation won't make you like other people – it will make you like *you*: the real you.

Beyond the mind chatter is everything that you want.

Despite what you may have read, 10–15 minutes a day is often not enough to still the mind, especially when you are new to it. That is like putting a snow globe down for three seconds and wondering why there's still snow everywhere; it hasn't settled yet. On the *Higher Power List* you did earlier, you might want to write on the right-hand side "Show me how long to meditate for" and see what comes to you. After doing this, people usually get an idea of how long – be it 30 minutes or 45 minutes or longer. And yes, sometimes it *is* 10–15 minutes, but rarely. That's often wishful thinking. If you are not sure how long to do, begin with 25 minutes.

When to Meditate

The best time to meditate is in the morning, just after you wake up. At this time, you might be possessed by the garbage mind chatter that takes you round and round in a very narrow circle. Or you can get out of that loop and into your Real Self. And that's why you meditate: to choose the latter option.

Meditation simply means focusing on something that isn't thinking – something which holds your attention away from your mind chatter. By that, I mean a focus that doesn't intellectually stimulate you; it doesn't get you into thinking. It doesn't matter what it is. And you may find that, for you, it doesn't have to be the sit-down type I am about to share, but that's a good starting point which works for many. You may discover that cleaning or gardening can be the focal point for your meditation practice. Or it could be the weights you lift at the gym – that becomes your focal point. In these cases, the actions you do become a focal point – a sound or your breath – to hold you, like an anchor.

The lower-self mind keeps itself in power by thinking all day.

The mind wants to be intellectually stimulated – all the time. So, it will play up when you focus on something that deprives it of this stimulation. It will calm after a while – so keep persevering through it. That's why meditation is so difficult for people – focusing on something that holds your focus out of thoughts is something the lower-self mind doesn't want to do because thoughts keep it activated and in charge.

How to Do *Focal-point Meditation*

1. Get into a comfortable position where you can relax but stay alert. Sit in a comfortable chair which keeps you upright. Or sit on the floor, cross-legged, perhaps with your back supported by a wall. Set a timer for the amount of time you want to practice.
2. Put on a consistent sound – the audio of a waterfall, the wind, wildlife, for example. Natural sounds work well because they can evoke the Real Self/flow state. Or sit in silence, putting your attention on any constant and consistent background noise, like the sound of a fan. Sometimes music is created from that flow state, but make sure it has a steady note or rhythm for you to hold and focus on and isn't too complicated, which may well get you

into analysing the music itself. I tend to use music which has a constant drone – a chord which plays through the piece, which I can focus on, but the music is less important to me than the fact there is a constant note throughout it.

3. With your eyes closed, in your mind's eye see a point of light like a star or a diamond – or some other image that appeals to you. Make sure the image won't get you further into thinking so keep it simple. One suggestion is the mast of a ship, especially when you are feeling anxious or something is going on that makes meditation a challenge. See it in your mind's eye – the mast of a ship in stormy seas – and hold on to it. The "waves" of thoughts can't touch you here. Stay holding the mast. Breathe into the image of this mast in your mind's eye and hold on to it like it's important. Keep coming back to the mast. Or your "go-to" image to hold in your mind's eye could be an anchor – picture a huge, solid metal ship's anchor. Way bigger than you, it represents stability and steadfastness.
4. Focus on the image and feel the sound connect with the image as if the sound is emanating from it. Give your full attention to the image; give yourself to the image, make it everything for this time of meditation.
5. Breathe into this image. Give your full attention to this image, your breath, and the sounds you can hear. Let your thoughts do their thing but be aware they are not you and nothing to do with you. Allow the snowstorm to happen as you stand back from your thoughts by focusing on the sound. It is usual for even more thoughts to try to tempt you away from your focus – interesting things as well as annoying things, all kinds of topics. The key is to keep coming back to your breath and the sound and the image.
6. Keep going. Give the focal point you are holding (be it your breath, the sound or the visual image, or the point of light in your mind's eye) your undivided attention. Give it full authority. Do it like it is essential, as though you'll get a reward at the end of it.

7. Every time your mind wanders into the snowstorm of thoughts, come back to your breath, breathing into the sound, and using the sound to breathe into and hold your focus. The only thing that matters right now is the focal point you are choosing to focus on. It has everything you want. You can trust it fully. Give the focal point more authority than your mind chatter. Imagine it as though you are staying with the nucleus of an atom and letting all the "electrons" of thoughts spin around. You remain centred, anchoring yourself with the breath and/or the image in your mind's eye. At some point, you will shift from focusing on the sound or image or breath to *being* the sound or image or breath – but that is not your work. It will happen when it happens, and it takes longer for some than others.
8. When the timer goes off, take a few deep breaths, slightly move your body and open your eyes.

Anchored in Your Real Self

Some people sit for their meditation and battle with thoughts for most of the time – if not all of the time, initially. This is OK, and it will go on for as long as it goes on for. You have been trained to think – and the mind wants to go into thoughts. It takes real focus sometimes not to. So "holding to your anchor" in meditation is not the easiest thing, but with practice, it will become easier.

I recommend doing *Focal-point Meditation* daily. Just like when you begin exercising – you may not see changes for weeks and months. It can be hard going and pointless seeming at the start, but you keep going. It takes practice. Meditation is a process of unhooking the lower-self mind. As you focus, the process takes over, and that mind chatter separates from you. This is not a process you can do yourself, but you get yourself into the position, focus, and then it happens when it happens.

> **Note:** If you are someone who thinks a lot and feels emotions strongly, meditation will be transformative for you. Because you are used to thinking a lot, don't be surprised if you resist – finding meditation incredibly dull – but that's even more reason to give it a go. This resistance, which is overthinking, is precisely the thing that's in your way and what meditation will sweep clear. But meditation does take practice to get good at, so don't get put off if you can't do it immediately.

Making Meditation Easier When the Snow Globe is Too Stormy

If you're finding it hard to get into meditation, you might want to do some physical exercise or stretching, before you begin. This can be an effective preparation for meditation, especially during those times when your mind seems too "snow stormy" to focus. Exercise can become a dynamic anchor to hold you centred and out of thoughts. Also, before you sit down to meditate, you might find this quick exercise helpful.

1. Sitting with your eyes closed, in your mind's eye, see a clear bubble forming around you.
2. Inflate this bubble.
3. As the bubble expands, allow it to push away all your thoughts, so you're left in the bubble.
4. Visualize the clear sides of the bubble. You can see outside, but all the noise and thoughts are outside; it's just total silence and tranquillity within – the volume is on mute. Expand the bubble to a comfortable size – a cosy pod or as big as a house. Once you've expanded the bubble to fit you, meditate in this tranquil space.

Once you are familiar with meditation, the practice itself will create a forcefield or aura around you, and you won't need to "activate" it so much through this exercise.

Suggested Practice for the Next Seven Days

Write "daily meditation" on the left-hand side of your *Higher Power List* to remind yourself, and in brackets write the length of time you are going to meditate for. When you've done your meditation, tick this off. Over this next week, begin your day with *Focal-point Meditation* and then remember to write down whatever comes up to surrender onto the right-hand side of the *Higher Power List.*

Once you have learned the techniques, it is a good idea to practice them every day. The morning is the best time if you can because it is very much about preparing for the day ahead. Though if that's absolutely not an option with time, people find success in the evenings, also. It is not like the gym where you require rest days; you can do this every day, workdays and the weekend. Use this first week to become practised in *Focal-point Meditation* and the *Higher Power List*, preparing for the course ahead.

Now, I'm going to share with you some things you can do to help yourself when going through challenging emotions.

Emotional Overwhelm Tools and Practices

When you are in the middle of a storm of overthinking and challenging emotions, you probably won't feel like writing, and you find it near-impossible to meditate. In fact, you might not feel like doing anything, but these soothing practices can help.

When you've gone into the type of overthinking that causes a really low mood, start by letting yourself have the bad moment you are having. It is OK, and it's a workout. Nothing has gone wrong. You can experience the workout while applying the following gentle practices. The key is to be gentle with yourself. Trying to fix or change is not loving. Trying to be positive right now or feel great right now is well-intentioned, but it can be abusive and harsh – it's saying that you're not doing good enough. Where you are is exactly where you are supposed to be, and all shall be well.

When those challenging emotions come up, you can follow these simple exercises – see which one appeals to you and perhaps

It is OK to feel not so good. It is OK to feel as you feel. Let yourself be. Let yourself overthink – and love yourself anyway.

put on some relaxing music in the background and begin. Don't do these techniques while driving or operating equipment. They are best done when you are at home, as they require sitting or lying down.

1. Focusing on Your Breath

The breath is always with you and deserves to be given more attention than your thinking. Your instant reaction to this statement may be to think that there's nothing in the breath, whereas thoughts have so much information within them. The opposite is true as you have learned – the breath gives you access to guidance from your Real Self – and thoughts are mostly "hot air". It is accurate to say you are your breath much more than you are your thoughts. Thoughts are not who you are and lead you nowhere. They are fictional stories which cloud your Real Self. There is great wisdom in the breath – or rather, the breath will lead you to that great wisdom, which arises in the silence. You can't find answers in the storms of the mind – so go to the breath, instead.

1. Bring your focus to your breath, breathing in through your nose, and out through the mouth or nose.
2. Slow down your breathing and make sure it is steady and consistent.
3. Hold to the inhale, hold to the exhale. Hold to the breath. Inhale for a count of five, exhale for a count of five. You don't need to go into thoughts right now. You don't need anything. All you need now is the breath. Hold to it. When you get used to this, you can increase to, for example, six or eight counts per inhale and six or eight counts per exhale. See what works for you.

Focusing on your breath like it matters creates space for new ideas and insights to come in as you are brought out of the storm and into the light of the Real Self. Don't overthink it – just breathe.

2. Focus on the Body

Panicky feelings can give an almost out-of-body feeling of being detached from yourself. To come back to the present, put your hands under warm water and massage the water over your hands and forearms. This brings your attention out of your thoughts and into your body. A warm shower also works. Physical exercise also works well. Alternatively use the following exercise in which you send love to each part of your body from your toes to the top of your head.

1. Lie down somewhere comfortable – and close your eyes.
2. Start by focusing on all of your body, really feeling a feeling of thankfulness as you do so.
3. Then bring to mind your toes. Send this area love, saying aloud or in your mind: "I love my toes, I love the soles of my feet, I love my heels, I love the tops of my feet, I love my ankles…"
4. Keep going all the way up to your head. As you do, imagine a ray of white or rainbow light moving up your body as you focus, moving through the parts you are loving.
5. See the rays of light beautifying and energizing you to a cellular level all the way up to your head. If you get distracted, begin the process all over again (beginning with your toes) and keep going until you have completed it.
6. Take a deep breath in and out and then open your eyes.

3. Take a Power Nap

If nothing else is working and you can do so, set a timer for 10–15 minutes and have a nap. Your mind chatter might resist by saying, "What a waste of time!" But do it anyway because it is a powerful way to "reboot" your mood. You may want to continue napping when you wake after 10 or so minutes so set the timer for another 10 minutes. However, it's best to avoid setting the timer for too much longer, as a deeper sleep may leave you feeling groggy. With short power naps, you will feel awake, energized and ready for the rest of your day.

Go with the Flow of Emotions
Rapids Float

This next process is useful if you're feeling anxious or overwhelmed or can't sleep and it works particularly well if you are engulfed with overthinking and emotions, that kind of mood when you feel an anxious feeling in your solar plexus/belly area. Perhaps you're lying awake, and you're just thinking round in circles. Many people tell me the *Rapids Float* helps them to drift off to sleep.

Anxiety is often due to bracing yourself against the waves of anxiety coming at you and trying to get rid of them or stop them coming. You might spend hours spinning in that emotional whirlwind or lie awake trying *not to* think or feel, but it's like fighting the flow of where you are, however well-meaning. The more you fight against the thoughts and feelings, the more they come at you, like waves (what you resist, persists). But let yourself be you – it is OK and understandable to do this if that's what you are doing right now.

Sometimes, you don't feel like writing or reading or doing much at all, so grab a pillow and relax into the thoughts and feelings.

Once you are engulfed in emotion, you can't just "feel good", so your options are to relax and float or fight. Any resistance means battling yourself, so your best choice is to float your way to find peace and silence.

Using the *Rapids Float*

1. Grab a pillow and hold it against your solar plexus, your belly – or whichever area you are feeling this emotional

reaction – perhaps the chest area. Just holding the cushion will give you some soothing.

2. Imagine the pillow is a float – a water buoyancy aid, like a life raft.
3. Hold the float. Feel the emotions coming at you and hold the float. Know that you will be OK because the float will keep you safe. The cushion acts as a float – so you can know that you will be fine to let the wave of emotion take you along with it.
4. See yourself holding the float with the storm waters coming at you. Let go into the flow of the storm or the negative emotions, knowing you are safe.
5. Relax into the feelings. Hold the float and go with the flow. No matter how big the waves are, you have the float. You are free to relax into the current. No matter how fast the current is, you will be OK. Hold onto the float and know that you are safe. Hold on and let the waves take you.
6. Don't try to get out of those feelings too quickly – that's not your job. Perhaps there is something here for you in them. Stay with them. Dive deep into them. Face the waves, holding the float.
7. Remember to breathe slowly and deeply through the process.
8. Repeat over and over: "I love myself for feeling [*name exactly how you feel – insomnia, fear, anxiety, jealousy – whatever it is*]." Forget how weird this seems and just repeat the words. After all, you won't feel like you "love" any of it, quite the opposite! These words just represent a willingness to go with the flow of however you're feeling. Repeat the sentence, over and over, imagine the current taking you and relax into it as best you can.
9. If you are in bed and can't sleep, close your eyes, grab the float and repeat this phrase imagining being taken along by the rapids knowing you are safe. It will help you drift off to sleep and remember this isn't about changing your thoughts or feelings, it's just about relaxing into the thoughts and feelings that you are in.

Be gentle with yourself like you would be to a friend that you loved – which is to be OK with what is going on right now, which includes the emotions. Say aloud or in your mind, "It's OK to feel this way. Thank you for this sensation. There's absolutely no rush, I can feel this way all night if I need to."

You can also do a variation of this process while travelling as a passenger, for example on a bus or train. Instead of the cushion, you can use a coat, sweater or rucksack. Close your eyes, hold the "float" and do the process.

Utilizing "Intrusive" Thinking to Your Advantage

Icon Switch

A sailing boat doesn't fight the wind but uses it to its advantage. And that is what we are going to do with this technique – use the intrusive thoughts to your advantage, which can be helpful if you are experiencing obsessive, repetitive thoughts or can't stop thinking about someone or something.

Intrusive thoughts are a huge problem, and you can see this by the fact that there are thousands of pages and dozens of forums on the internet all about how to stop overthinking. But it is an uphill struggle, because the more you try *not to think* of these thoughts, the more you think about them. The problem is calling these thoughts "unwanted" or "negative" empowers them. As you now know, when we resist, we lose. Trying to slam the door on these thoughts seems to invite more of them and before you know it, you are surrounded – obsessing about them and trying to get rid of them – they multiply – and the cycle continues.

And so, your thinking mind keeps going back into the thoughts, regardless of how much you don't want to do this, analysing who said what and why etc. Or it ruminates on the fear thoughts, keeping picturing that situation that you are afraid of. It is like it goes over and over the subjects, hoping to find a solution – but it never does. Solutions are not to be found in the snowstorm of mind chatter.

First, know that what you are doing is OK. This is normal. This is how the mind works. Nothing is going to go wrong – in fact, all this overthinking is just a workout of the clearer mind which is to come. But now, you are going to find a new way to look at it – a way to meet with those "intrusive" thoughts that will give you freedom, finally, from these thoughts having power over you.

The Benefit of Obsessive Thinking

Imagine doing push-ups (or other exercises) and not knowing the gains they were creating. You would see it as tiring and pointless. If you spent hours at the gym and thought it was all about the tension with no positive result – of course, you'd resist it. But once you understand the gains – that this tension creates something good for you – you can get excited with every push-up that you do. In fact, the more, the better. They might be an effort when you do them, but you'll happily go through this tension and do them because of the gains they are creating. The gains aren't so easy to see with our "workout" of thoughts – where most people only focus on the tension, and they don't even know about gains. As a result, they fight against their workout, and the whole experience becomes horrible. But there is no difference with these examples. Your "intrusive" thoughts – in fact, all thinking – are the same as weights at the gym: they cause tension and also gains.

Every time you keep thinking of that person or situation, it is actually a good thing. Rather than see it as an intrusive thought to get rid of, welcome it in – it is a "push-up". That's how you want to see it. And what if these intrusive thoughts are not intrusive/unwanted at all, but a weight coming your way? This is exciting as the more "weightlifting" you do, the better the gains that are coming are. So, in one way, the more thoughts, the better.

And so, as unusual as this may sound, let yourself think about the person or the situation if that's what you are doing anyway. I'm not saying *try to* think intrusive thoughts. But if you are thinking them already, go with them – and visualize a push-up with each one. The push-up is what I call your "icon" – which we will come to in a minute. So, you can see how you can get almost excited about the overthinking, now you know there is a positive gain related to it. As I said, these "unwanted" thoughts are not unwanted at all – they are an opportunity to do push-ups – which will bring you great benefits.

How to *Icon Switch*

While working out at the gym, you might get a flash of an image of the gain: you imagine the benefits of weightlifting with improved chest and arms, for example. Yes, you feel the tension, but that is not the main event, because you're focused on the gains. And so, you want to create an image that represents the gains rather than the challenging workout: a more dynamic "go to" image.

You can create the same focus for your thoughts. I refer to this as an "icon" because you use an image of the gain in your mind to overlay the intrusive thoughts. An icon is a still image – or it could be a short scene, like a video image of a few seconds – a GIF, in other words. So, look for an image that best-represents the diametric opposite of the overthinking. The gains of push-ups are toned, strong muscles – so what could the gain of this thought be? It might be vague, so if someone was unkind to you, your icon could be friendly, interesting people around you in a lavish setting – perhaps at a party or event. This is what you use for your split-second image or GIF.

The mind likes excitement, so make the icon vivid – a still of money or a prize of something, perhaps. It could be something attractive or affluent and appealing to you. It could be the image of you on a beach, looking great, confident and living an incredible life.

You don't have to put that person or situation who has let you down or is causing you to worry into the overlay; instead, choose a totally new person or situation – the opposite to what the thoughts are about. If someone is aggressive toward you and you keep thinking about it, make your overlay image about you surrounded with strong, attractive, loving people at your side. If you are facing redundancy, your overlay image might be the image of you in a fantastic new workplace. You are looking for the gains of these thoughts rather than the tension. If your mind keeps going over a critical or unkind comment, you could switch to an image of someone likeable telling you how amazing you are or complimenting you in some specific way. Every time that person or situation or other annoying thoughts come to mind, don't fight the thoughts, just overlay it with the "go-to" image.

Harnessing Overthinking

Every time you think of the person or the situation you don't want to think about, flash up and "overlay" the image on top of it. Just as when doing physical press-ups, you see an image flashing of the gains – deliberately do this in this circumstance, too – flash-up your icon. It's not about trying not to think of the intrusive thought – it's about overlaying the image of the gains. Tell yourself you will get a reward if you spend enough time focusing on the new image or icon. You could even make the image like a GIF of winning the jackpot, gold coins water falling out of a machine or an equivalent scene of abundance. The more you practice your icon, the more real it will become for you and have more vividness than that repetitive thought or worry.

Keep doing push-ups – it's not about stopping the thoughts; they are your friends. They are evolving you. They are creating your dreams. So, go with the push-ups and overlay the image.

The *Icon Switch* is not about denying what happened to you but preventing the unpleasant thought replays in your mind by replacing them with something truer. In other words, you start to see the situations happening to you as workouts with benefits rather than problems. It is an incredible way to get thoughts of that person or situation you want to forget about totally out of your mind so you can get on with your life!

Dealing with Worry About Other People

Every time a worrying thought comes up about someone else, see a prayer going to them or the image of them surrounded with helpers or guides – and the "gain" of the situation happening instead. If you keep thinking the same thoughts – what if that's necessary right now for a specific result for them, like when you keep on weightlifting your arms for bigger arms? So, go with it – *worry thoughts* about them create *power thoughts* about them. Just like push-ups are actually beneficial and necessary for getting the improvements – what if these thoughts are, too. Don't try to get out of your workout too quickly, in other words. Be with it.

The more you use the *Icon Switch*, the more natural and automatic it will become – and you will almost look forward to the previously "unwanted" thoughts coming, knowing they are push-ups containing a gift or gain for you. After some practice, the process will become automatic, and you will be more open to the intrusive thoughts, which means you will not be so wrapped up in them. At this point, you won't need to do the process so much, but it's always there if you need it.

Once you become accustomed to using the *Icon Switch* and it becomes almost automatic, you may want to use the *Thought Neutralizer* described below to keep your mind secure and clear of general overthinking, sort of like maintenance. These techniques offer different approaches, but through experimenting, you will discover which tool works best for you in which situation.

Clearing Your Surroundings of Unwanted Thoughts

Thought Neutralizer

The *Thought Neutralizer* is where you say "thank you" aloud, under your breath or in your mind and use it as a space clearing spray or spray filled with love. It's one to use when thinking about things you don't want to think about, or thoughts are circling and threatening to make an appearance.

Every time the unwanted thoughts come near – meaning the intrusive person or situation comes to mind – meet it with the declaration "thank you". In your mind's eye, aim the "spray" at the thoughts or image and mentally say "thank you" with every spray. Just repeat the words in your mind "thank you" at the image that's coming to mind, be it an unpleasant subject or invented conversation or scenario with that person you don't want to think about. The thought comes in, you repeat "thank you" and picture yourself aiming the spray at whatever the subject is, be it person, place or thing. It comes in again, and it is "thank you, thank you".

Repeat "thank you" like a mantra, over and over and over, spraying every time. Repeat it like you are holding a disinfectant, and you are spraying it out in front of you, neutralizing the thoughts and clearing your path, cleansing the entire room. Every time a thought approaches, spray it down. You are getting rid of intrusive thoughts before they take hold as if they are weeds.

We use the word "thank you" because these words assume the highest Real Self perspective where everything – including all situations and even thoughts – are on your side. So, the only right response is "thank you", even if you can't see why at the time. Even if your perspective is that it seems to be the complete opposite. Remember, it is not about *feeling* thankful – you just say the words, in your mind. With every "thank you" you "spray" to obliterate the unwanted thoughts or images. This clears the atmosphere and clears your path

Note: If you have intense unwanted thoughts, this "space clearer" may not be powerful enough to win-out against intense thoughts. It would be like spraying air freshener over the top of a dirty or messy house, and it can get you to battle your thoughts, seemingly giving them power. If that's the case, use the *Icon Switch* instead – which is like a deep clean – and will get you into the habit of going with the thoughts rather than resisting them. It will disempower the intrusive thoughts enough for the *Thought Neutralizer* to work. Once you get good at this, the *Thought Neutralizer* can be applied to prevent the intrusive thoughts from taking hold.

Some people have found that adding-on words to the "thank you" declaration helps. For example, "thank you for this healing" if the unwanted thought is about health worries for yourself or a loved one. Or "thank you for my great life" if the subject of thought is general pessimism. Or "thank you for my wealth" as you spray down a thought about personal or even world poverty. In other words, you go to the "gain" opposite and speak the words of that. As always – experiment and find out what works for you.

- Hand over all those thoughts, your desires, your concerns, your dilemmas on to the right-hand side of the *Higher Power List.* Offload all that mind chatter and thinking and focus on the actions you will take to centre yourself.
- Learn to focus as your mind settles with *Focal-point Meditation.*
- Choosing to give undivided attention to your breath or the body takes your attention away from your thoughts, centring you and clearing your mind.
- If none of the other practices in this section are working, take a power nap. This will give you a "reset" as you awaken renewed and refreshed with another chance to begin the day again, at any time of day.
- Use *Rapids Float* to relax into the flow of whatever emotion you are in. Use when you're overwhelmed, or at night when you can't sleep due to overthinking.
- Use the *Icon Switch* when you can't get a compulsive problematic thought of someone or something out of your mind. Switch to the "gains" side of the workout.
- Use *Thought Neutralizer* to keep circling thoughts at bay.

WEEK 2

FREEDOM

Keep on going – results will happen in time. Keep on handing over what's on your mind on your *Higher Power List* and doing *Focal-point Meditation.*

Last week was all about identifying what is going on with your life right now and how you would like things to be different. Over the following week, you will be combining two daily practices from Week 1 – your *Higher Power List* (see page 36) and *Focal-point Meditation* (see page 40) with the new tools of this section.

A common question about meditation that often comes up around now is, "Why don't I feel any different?" But like going to the gym, it may take longer than a week before you see results. Keep going anyway, even if your mind chatter tells you it is not working. This is normal – keep going anyway. This is also a good time to check that you are spending enough time meditating because as I said 10–15 minutes often isn't enough – especially if you tend to overthink. If you feel like that's the case, increase the time you spend in meditation.

With meditation, what works is doing it and doing it for long enough.

As you continue into Week 2, you'll be expanding the list of tools on the left-hand side of your Higher Power List to create a daily routine. You'll be doing this over the coming weeks. Remember it's not your job to think about the right-hand side of the list. Throw all those questions, thoughts and desires on the right-hand side of the list. Anytime you feel overwhelmed, drop it over on the right-hand side and then get on with your job – those tools to clear your mind and centre you. You may think you don't have enough time in your schedule, but these are practical tools that don't have to take up that much time in the morning, and then you'll have the rest of the day free. The clear-minded state you'll get from doing them will give you more time to get things done and enjoy your day.

This week, you'll be focusing on what's blocking you because when you don't feel as good as you'd like, it's usually due to overthinking. This could be because there is a desire in the way or you're unconsciously resisting. The *Higher Power List* will help you hand over your desires and problems, while *Focal-point Meditation* clears them from your mind and will help you overcome overthinking in time. The tools this week, the *"What's Good About…" List* and the *Freedom Process*, will help you let go of those subjects you find hard to forget, no matter how hard you try. Together these practices will release you from wanting to change something or push something away. You will discover the doorway to your freedom and the doorway to what you want.

> Techniques and tools are marked with and are introduced over the four-week course. It's a good idea to find time for at least three practices a day but do what works best for you. At the end of the course, on page 119, you'll find a chart of all the tools and practices covered, which you can use to create your own personalized daily plan.

Freedom to Appreciate

It's not always possible to "get rid" of your blocks by reading or workshopping. These methods might help you to articulate your blocks – but they are unlikely to disappear as a result. The following practice, however, is radical in that it will help you to see the challenges your mind is trying to escape as an untapped goldmine. Once you have applied the *"What's Good About..." List* and the *Freedom Process* then you can move on to dwelling on all the good in your life. Then you'll realize why the seemingly simple "gratitude list" promoted by so many personal development teachings doesn't always work so well. Probably because it's difficult to "count your blessings" when your mind is clouded by overthinking. As you find a way to navigate your blocks, it will free you up to move into that space where gratitude and appreciation become natural and effortless, and you'll recall all those memories of confidence with the *Confidence Evoke.*

Embracing All of You

"What's Good About..." List

Focusing on those parts of yourself you've probably been avoiding, let's start with a question: "Are you able to embrace *all* parts of yourself – and *all* the parts of your life?"

Sometimes, we deny parts of ourselves, and it becomes such a habit we don't even know we are doing it. Pause for a moment: Are you embracing your looks, your personality quirks, your talents, your voice and your mannerisms, for example? All those unique and beautiful parts of yourself that make you, you. Often those parts we don't like about ourselves are the ones we expect others to compliment to make us feel good – and then we feel surprised and annoyed when they don't. We forget that life is a mirror of how we feel about ourselves and that it is *our* job to unconditionally accept ourselves first.

What Feelings Have You Been Avoiding?

So how are you *really* feeling right now? You might want to feel confident and happy, but find yourself engulfed by thoughts and the emotions that go with that, so you really only have two choices right now:

1. Settle in to and accept where you are and how you are feeling right now, or
2. Fight where you are and how you are feeling right now.

The first of these two choices will move you to the place you want to be. We cringe when it comes to admitting to ourselves that we feel lonely, needy, or insecure. There is something about those specific emotions and similar ones that make us do anything rather than face them just as they are. But I want you to face these feelings – and then begin to make friends with them.

Everyone gets embarrassed about feeling lonely or needy or sad. You feel how you feel, and it's OK. It may even be how you are meant to be feeling right now. You don't have to feel perfectly positive all the time and, in fact, that wouldn't evolve you. So, you don't need to deny or escape your feelings too quickly; let them work on you, as they may be important for your evolution right now.

Trying to get out of them too soon keeps us more stuck in them. It's like trying to sprint while attached to a rubber band: it keeps bringing you back to the start, and you get ever more defeated and tired on every attempt until the feeling overwhelms you. Accepting these emotions, snuggling in with them even, is self-honouring and will unhook you from the rubber band so-to-speak and frees you to accept that you'll feel better in the perfect time. Tell yourself, "I am willing to feel my intensity, I am willing to be worked on." Stay with the feelings, face them, be with them, be with the storm and stay with it.

You are meant to feel how you feel right now – this should be happening because it is.

It may sound strange to be OK with a mood when it doesn't feel good. But much of this feeling is the effects of resisting the mood; it has little to do with the mood itself. Anxiety is one thing when you are (understandably) judging it and trying to get out of it, and a totally different feeling when you're going with the flow of it – befriending it even. Your mind fights anything it doesn't want, and that's the problem because what you resist persists. But even this isn't a problem ultimately because, remember: The resistance is resistance training – and evolves your best life.

When you are in this state, it's important to realize that appearances "out there" are just a temporary mirror of your inner state. This is because when your thoughts are stormy, your whole experience is likely to adjust to your mood. For example, you may not like what you see in the mirror and wonder why you are looking so unattractive. This illusion, again, which is your own perception, is a sure sign that you are out of centre right now. It takes practice to remember this – that it is a temporary mirror rather than a fixed reality.

When we get taken over by an emotional wave, we seem to merge with it; we seem to become one with it; we become the emotion. If this is the case – and it always is if you are feeling overwhelmed by emotion – then to love yourself, you must love the emotion. You see, if you don't love the emotions you're experiencing, then you don't love yourself in this moment either. And this is how you become free of it. Accepting and befriending the feeling dismantles it and frees us from it. It's that paradox that says: To change something, you must first accept it exactly as it is.

How to Use the *"What's Good About…" List*

The *"What's Good About…" List* is about being open to life, trusting that what is coming at you is supposed to and it is your work to find the gift in it. You might find the process difficult to begin with, as your mind is probably so used to looking for bad things about everything, so make sure you feel relaxed and comfortable before starting and bear in mind it may take some time before you "get it".

"*What's Good About* How You're Feeling?"

Let's say you feel scared or sad or isolated or lonely. Usually, no one wants to admit these things. But now you are not only going to face how you feel but write "*What's Good About* this feeling". For example:

- *This uncomfortable feeling is a nudge to do the inner work; it's forcing me to go within and discover my power. Perhaps I need this feeling to encourage me to do my daily practices.*
- *Considering my background, I should be feeling this way, and anyone would feel this way in this situation.*
- *It's OK to feel as I do. Perhaps I'm meant to be feeling this, or thinking these thoughts, to evolve my life to where I want to go.*
- *This is a new experience I am going through, and a workout. This feeling is a sign that I'm evolving – and gains will come in afterwards.*
- *This intense feeling shows that I care. Maybe I need this powerful thrust to create a solution? I'm on track, so this must be a right response.*

"*What's Good About* Fearing What People Think?"

One of the biggest obstacles to living our best life is the fear of what other people think. So first, you want to accept that. Trying to not care what people think when you *do* care is resistance and will keep you stuck. For example:

- *Caring what people think has some good in it because it shows that I do care about people and their feelings; I am a caring, kind person.*
- *Considering my background, it's understandable I'm scared about what other people think – so I'm actually doing really well to get where I now am on this subject.*
- *Maybe I'm deliberately bothered about what people think so that I can work out the opposite – which is being myself no matter what people think.*

"*What's Good About* Apathy or Emptiness?"

We sometimes feel apathy or an empty feeling when we have ambition. Of course, you are going to occasionally feel a longing –

a gap – because what you are wanting doesn't seem to be happening right now. Plus, it's a sign of your workout. Everyone I've worked with – and I have worked with some very materially successful people – has felt this along the way to making their dreams a reality. This longing is a sign that what you want is coming; it's a sign of your ambition. If you didn't have this feeling it means you don't want it enough – so it's a very good sign. For example:

- *This is a void to be filled in with something new and exciting.*
- *This apathy is a workout for passion, and it's calling for more excitement in my life. The feeling is also showing me how far I've come – because I used to feel this all the time, and now I don't.*
- *Other people are dealing with this too, right now, so many other people are going through this – everyone has these kinds of days. Perhaps in my own way, I am somehow leading the way for others, too, because I am a leader.*

"*What's Good About* Being Controlling?"

One of the biggest confusions when we call someone "controlling" is that, in reality, not many people actually want to control someone else – why would they? It's too much work, and it doesn't work because it just makes you feel controlled. Instead, they want to clear their mind and be in their Real Self, like everyone does. For example:

- *Well, I am often accurate about what's best for people and situations and so I'm coming from a place of leadership and sharing my guidance rather than criticizing.*
- *It shows leadership skills – all leaders have the tendency to be called controlling on the way to them becoming great leaders.*
- *It shows strength of character – at least I make an impact, and I'm seen as a powerful person.*

"*What's Good About* Doubt?"

Whenever you move out of your comfort zone to try something new, doubt is a high possibility. And this is a good sign – it is the workout for doubt's opposite, which is belief. For example:

- *Doubt is the workout for more faith and belief. Even the most trusting people experience doubt, as doubt is a necessary weightlift for trust.*
- *I should be feeling this because I am. I'm going to let this feeling work on me.*
- *Doubt is a part of the journey on the way to what I want. It's a sign that I'm moving out of my comfort zone into my best life. It's a sign that good is coming.*

"*What's Good About* Having a Bad Day?"

Trying to turn a bad day into a good one often makes it worse and trying to escape, heal or change your mood – to change a bad day to a good day – equals resistance. Self-acceptance is the balm you are looking for. It's OK to have a bad day and be vulnerable sometimes. Just as you endure at the gym – you don't give in at the first signs of tension – realize that feeling bad or having a bad day is just a sign of your workout. Gains are coming when the storm clouds clear. For example:

- *Everyone has a bad day sometimes. It is OK to feel as I do. This is how you evolve good days. This is a detox and a nudge to up my practice and change my schedule.*
- *It is OK to have a bad day. It is showing me how far I've come – I used to feel this way all the time.*
- *I'm going to write off the day as a "bad day". Everyone has these days. I'm going to settle into it and make friends with it.*

"*What's Good About* Shame?"

Shame is relentless self-criticism and the opposite of loving who you are. But remember, shame is also beneficial because it evolves self-love and self-empowerment (which is the opposite of shame). Yes – *it's a workout.* Embracing your shame is one of the most powerful ways to let it go. Letting yourself unconditionally overthink something (if that's what you're doing anyway) is your way out of it. So, you just want to accept yourself, and watch the thoughts and feelings you don't want leave you and the ideas and feelings you do want come into your experience. For example:

- *It is OK to feel shame – it's a very common feeling, and I can be with it and let it evolve me knowing it will pass.*
- *It is a workout for self-love. It's a workout for being confident about who I am. It's a workout to not care what people think.*
- *Some of the people who felt the most shame are now those people who are the freest and are totally being them.*

Self-love means loving all parts of yourself. When you love yourself fully, you release what isn't working and increase what is working. No harm can ever come from loving yourself.

Dealing with Challenging Situations

It might be hard to believe, but when you welcome an unwanted thought or feeling, it leaves. This isn't about action at all. You are accepting the idea and the impulse to *want* to act out. Often when you've embraced the thought or feeling, you find you simply don't want to act on it anyway. In other words, you love the feeling of being angry, for example, rather than thinking that this means to express it. And, in fact when you love it, you are much less likely to express it.

When you're dealing with a challenging situation – or a situation that has only recently happened and is still intensely on your mind – first you want to write "*What's Good About* my reaction" before going into "*What's Good About* the situation itself". You can also use the term *"What's OK About…"* instead if that feels more realistic.

For example: If you feel intensely worried when you look at your bank statement, don't go straight to "*What's Good About* not having much money". Start by identifying how you are feeling. Let's say you realize you feel fear. First, you face the mood, just as it is. For example:

- *It's OK to feel this – everyone would feel this in my situation.*
- *Feeling worried shows I've got the ambition for money (which is necessary). I can imagine all wealthy people have felt this; it's also showing me I have self-respect (some people wouldn't care at all, which may not be so good).*

Now you can move into "*What's OK About* having less money":

- *Having less money is a workout; it's "calling in" money.*
- *It's getting me to budget and shop around and buy different kinds of things, for now, some of which are really good – and this budgeting is helping me in other areas of life.*
- *It has really honed what I want – which is a really great lifestyle and got me to look into new avenues to bring in money, which feels exciting.*

First, embrace the emotion about the situation, then you can embrace the situation itself. Loving yourself means loving your thoughts, loving your emotions – all of it. "Today, I feel like a failure, and that's fine." There's a particular power in accepting those things that are seemingly the opposite of where you want to be. Where you are is not forever and when you look for "*What's Good About...*" and knowing it's just for today – not forever – you can do this process more easily.

Finding the Gains in the Workout Freedom Process

The "*What's Good About...*" *List* is incredibly powerful and becomes more so with practice – and you want to keep going with that. In some circumstances, though – especially initially – it might feel like you are not able to find the good in certain issues. For those situations, I'd like to introduce you to the

Freedom Process, where you jump straight into loving where you are. This process quickly (and sometimes instantly) transforms the negative into a positive that you can understand and believe in and even *love*, right now.

As you now know, every situation is a workout in disguise. You see, you can't *really* love where you are if you don't know about the gains. It's like being expected to love the tension at the gym, without knowing that it creates muscle – that the weightlifting has a purpose.

To take this gym analogy further. If you want to create a particular quality, you will go to this "Gym of Life", and you would tell the trainer what it is you wanted to develop, for example, more confidence. So, they'd hand you a weight called "insecurity". Initially, you might be wondering why you were handed insecurity when you asked for confidence – but then you would hear insecurity is the weight that creates confidence.

Money challenges create wealth. I have never met a financially rich person who hasn't either been extremely poor or at least felt it and gone into intense fear thoughts about poverty. These weights or challenges are a *necessary* part of the journey. Before long you'll get to a place when you can say confidently "Bring it on." Every challenge is a gift which as you love it will turn to your advantage, hugely benefiting your life. So, you *want* to encounter these weights; you want to actually choose them. Choosing them rather than fighting them is the way to your freedom. As you love and accept the "weightlifting" part of your journey, you supercharge your way to the gains.

Every challenge has a corresponding gain.

How to Do the *Freedom Process*

Get a piece of paper and write on the left-hand side in the top left corner "workout/weights" and on the right-hand side in the top right corner write "gift/gains".

Under the left-hand side heading, you are going to list those feelings or situations coming up at the moment that keeps you from feeling fully empowered and in your Real Self. It could be a longstanding issue – a theme that has gone on for years – or it could be a current feeling. Write what you're experiencing on the left. Just go for it, write down all those feelings – in one word or a sentence detailing how you feel and what's going on.

Now for the fun part. Once you've finished your list, on the right-hand list, you write the exact opposite. You are not trying to feel the feelings of these words – you're simply doing the process. It's technical, not emotional – just a task to be done, like answering an exam question. You are going to take some time to "opposite" every word and feeling you've just written, asking yourself as you do so, "What is this weight producing as a gain for me?" For example:

WORKOUT/WEIGHTS	(creates) >>>	**GIFT/GAINS**
Insecurity	>>>	Security, confidence
Fear	>>>	Fearlessness
Worry	>>>	Trust, optimism, happiness, excitement
Arguments	>>>	Great relationships
Feeling bored	>>>	Passion, enthusiasm
Overthinking	>>>	Clear-minded, focused, Zen-like
Worrying about problems	>>>	Excited about life
Not enough business	>>>	Fully booked appointments, big sales
Wanting to move	>>>	Perfect home, penthouse apartment
Don't like my job	>>>	A career I love, life purpose
Not recognized	>>>	Validated, celebrated
Bad day	>>>	Amazing day
Trying to be positive	>>>	Unshakeable faith
Imagining negative things	>>>	Positive outcome, blessings, miracles
Feeling weak	>>>	Feeling strong, powerful, beautiful

Remember these key points – these are your "Freedom Statements".

1. The fastest way to get to the gains is to embrace the weights.
2. You require the weights to get the "gains".

Loving the Weights Like a Bodybuilder

The way to get to where you want to be (the right-hand side) is to embrace where you are. So, the next thing you do is write "I love…" and then write the first thing on your list under workout/weights. Your choice is to accept what is going on now – or keep fighting it. The biggest reason of all to love these feelings/situations is that they are evolving the best of you. You don't really need any other reason than that.

This process deconstructs those "enemies" – which are predominantly your own resistance to those things you call your blocks. When you use this process to love and appreciate them, they fall away as you realize they were never blocks, but weights that are on your side. So below what you've written so far, based on the diagram above, the list will look something like this:

- *I love feeling insecure.*
- *I love feeling fear.*
- *I love worrying.*
- *I love arguments.*
- *I love feeling bored.*

How can you love these seemingly unpleasant situations/feelings? It's because these are the weights *required* for the corresponding gain. You simply *have to* go through them to get to those gains – just like the bodybuilder has to go through the tension of weightlifting to get the muscles. The weight is something to be celebrated – it means you are on track and what you want is coming. Remember, you are not looking to change anything – you are simply embracing things as they are. That's it. Just making this list is enough for you to get a realization – a shift. What's more, with practice, this process will become easier and even automatic.

Freedom Process Journal

Another way of doing this process is to write down a paragraph in more detail about how you feel – like a journal entry. Just let the words flow. Now, you're going to go through it, reversing the words.

For example:

"Today, I felt absolutely terrible. I felt empty and bored with my life and just not knowing what decision to make next. I feel lost, and I have no idea what would make me happy or what steps to take. I don't feel like doing any hobbies. I just want to stay in bed all day."

Becomes:

"Today, I felt absolutely amazing. I felt fulfilled and excited about my life and full of ideas. I feel focused and excited about all these new interests of mine and can't wait to put them into practice. I can't wait to fully enjoy my life and all the exciting things that are going on for me."

Remember to read through your *Freedom Statements* to remind yourself why you are doing this process and the logic behind it. As I said, do the *Freedom Process* like you are doing a technical project – put your emotions aside and go through the whole piece of writing, finding the best reversal for it. You can apply this to your actual diary entries, and you will experience the freedom in realizing that everything you've gone through is not for nothing – it's creating your best life.

Appreciate Your Life
Gratitude 150

Both the practices this week have focused on appreciating where you are right now and being OK about it. Appreciation is a feeling which doesn't have any thoughts associated with it: it's a feeling of love. So as soon as you feel clear-minded about any issues and *"What's Good"* or *"What's OK"* about them, it's time to move on and focus on what's working in your life. If you can't quite get into this, go back to the *"What's Good About..." List* until you can. When you're OK with how you're feeling and what's going on right now, it's time to move from embracing your problems to embracing the good in your life. Gratitude expands your good – appreciation *appreciates.* In other words, if you want wealth, revel in the wealth you've got. If you want beauty, revel in the beauty you've got.

It can seem unsettling, but it's totally normal to feel "low" and/or face huge resistance to doing appreciation. As easy as this process seems, it is not. And that's why so many people give up the lists after just a short period of trying it (which isn't enough to experience effects). This drop is your workout and a sign to keep on going! You're on the brink of a shift for the better. If it's too difficult, begin with a *"What's Good About..." List* or meditate, for example.

Appreciation opens the door to the flow of ideas from your Real Self.

Desires are your ambitions which are the necessary workout to get you what you want. But once you've had them for a short while, they become an obstacle. Wanting something you haven't got stops you loving today. Keep a *Higher Power List* nearby, and every time a desire comes up, write it on the right-hand side. This way, you surrender your desires (*Higher Power List*) and then get on with living your day – and then use the other processes to help you accomplish this.

The key to making this list work for you is to choose "light" or childlike topics. Start with something trivial or simple like favourite items in the home or favourite items of clothing. For example:

- *I love my new outfit.*
- *I love my washbag and backpack.*
- *I love my home and the outlook over the park.*

- *I love my new gym membership.*
- *I love that bargain coat I picked up today.*
- *I love that the shop assistant smiled at me today and then deliberately came back and served me at the till especially.*

Go through those things you've got at home, things you bought such as clothes or technology that at one point "made your day" and now they're boring. Appreciate them. Bring them back to life. Doing this, you will rediscover that first-time feeling even more intensely than the first time and open the way to more of that. Rather than constantly wishing for your dream home, why not make where you are more of your dream home? The lower-self mind wants to race off into wanting something better all the time – instead, you want to get more excited about right now. This gratitude may very well lead you on to tidying up your home more, repainting or getting new furniture, which is a practical extension of gratitude.

Grateful for Being You – What Makes You Eligible?

Gratitude and appreciation extend to yourself too. You may not be exactly where you want to be, but no one wants to hire someone who's "waiting to be discovered" – they want to hire a star and you want to first discover yourself. Ask yourself, "What makes me eligible?" And write it down.

For example: "What makes [*insert your name here*] eligible…"

- *I've got an interesting job.*
- *I've got great eyes.*
- *I've got a nice voice.*
- *I dress well.*
- *I've got a great body.*

Some people might say that this type of appreciation is shallow – but finding something to hold your attention and pull you out of negative mind chatter is the access point to who you are, which is anything but shallow. This is all about getting inspired or sparking your excitement. Making a list of things you label deeper or more serious such as "I love the way the sun comes up every morning" may not work for you. Does it spark your interest as much as your new outfit, sofa, or friendships? It might do – and you may think it ought to do – but does it? Only you know the answer.

There are no rules on *what* to appreciate – it's what makes you feel good – and I've found that the simple is more often than not the route to connection. And it may be a really material focal point of love/appreciation that gets you in.

One of the things you'd do if you had it all – and you had more time in the day – is to *appreciate more.* Because this is a secret to happiness: being centred and being You – who appreciates by nature.

Renewing Appreciation for People, Places and Things

I remember coming to London for the first time: it was sunny and the buildings were so huge compared to where I'd come from. I felt an enthusiasm and anticipation about the place. When I moved there, the excitement faded, and it became more normal. When I used appreciation, I reignited the feeling and the city became new once again. In fact, I got that feeling back bigger than the first time, and this makes sense. All the time I had "gone off" the place, I was evolving more excitement and more adventure. My appreciation opened the door to my gains of love for the city. And you can do it with anything.

When you get a new outfit you feel great in, compliments soon come in. The compliments are simply agreeing with your own self-opinion about how great you look. And that is why often when you go off the outfit, so do other people and the compliments stop. You too can "renew" that first-time feeling.

Go to your wardrobe. Begin there. Go to those items that at one time thrilled you. And then go to those gadgets that you were thrilled about when they first came through the mail – and remind yourself what's great about them.

Reignite that "new in town" feeling.

I remember working with someone who increased her list to writing 150 things – and it really made her feel great, and her life started improving – and this is why this list is called *Gratitude 150.*

How to Do *Gratitude 150*

To write a list of 150 things you're grateful for takes time – and most people don't do it, for this reason. But making a list gives you the winning edge, I've found. When you get to 85 or so, you can almost run out of things to write. But stay with it. More insights will come, and you will start discovering more things to write and perhaps things you haven't remembered for a while.

When you do reach 150, you will find that you naturally look for the good in situations throughout the day. You will find yourself appreciating more, and so thinking less – because you can't think and appreciate at the same time. In this almost meditative state, you will hear your inner guidance rather than the static-in-the-radio of mind chatter. You can also choose a specific subject, for example, do "Looks 150" or "Career 150".

You can also write down all the people in your life – your loved ones, friends and family, and all the loveable things about them all. Write "I love…" and write all of their names, really feeling the appreciation.

Of course, you don't have to list 150 – sometimes you won't have time. But the number in the title will remind you to do more rather than less. Writing 50 things down rather than just saying five things in your mind, for example.

Loving Your Enemies Disarms *Them* and Empowers *You*

Love is the answer and opens the door to miracles. Gratitude clears the path. Love makes everything right, dissolving and disarming your enemies. Love is everything. Whether you call it love or gratitude or appreciation doesn't really matter – each word is so similar, and it's about the feeling not the label.

Gratitude creates a forcefield: a shield that allows you to glide over your problems and renders you powerful.

People never have obsessive unwanted thoughts about things they love. It's the "trying not to think" the thought that fuels the thought to the point of obsession; it's a thinking that "I shouldn't be thinking the thought I'm thinking". And so, unconditional love or appreciation is how to let go of obsession. Look for the good in the person, place or thing you want to forget about – and then fill your mind with other people, places, things and subjects that you find easy to appreciate.

Developing Confidence

Confidence Evoke

The value of being confident and developing confidence is clear, but how do you actually accomplish it? *Confidence Evoke* is a way to successfully develop confidence, step-by-step, through identifying times when you felt confident, and bringing them to mind. It's a simple way to practise these feelings more until it becomes our new normal. However, it is not about thinking confident thoughts – it's not about *thinking* at all. When you revisit memories of when you felt confident, you move into that non-thinking, clear-minded state. When you are confident, you are not in the state of thinking – you are *being*, untethered by thought. That's why it feels so amazing – you are in your Real Self state in these moments.

Often you might get a compliment and feel a momentary buzz… and then seconds later go off into mind chatter which probably includes an amount of self-criticism. Within a short time, the compliment is totally forgotten.

> Many people replay the critical mind chatter – but *Confidence Evoke* is about replaying the compliments and those moments when you felt self-confident instead.

Confidence Evoke is the opposite of that – in it, you actively dwell on compliments; you really get the most out of them. Compliments also include those times you feel good about yourself (which is giving yourself the compliment) – and so you dwell on these too until you are feeling great.

You may think you've never felt confident or received many compliments. But you have had many thousands or even millions of experiences or moments – and somewhere in there you have at least felt fleeting confidence, everyone has. This technique is about rediscovering and then revisiting those times. As you practise this technique, you will remember more and more times you have already felt the way you want to feel.

How to Do *Confidence Evoke*

Choose an area of life, for example, your body image, or your level of career success. In this example, we are going to use career success. On a piece of paper, write down a sentence or two – which I call your "Affirmative Statement" – which is a description of who you really are, without the thoughts in the way. This isn't trying to pretend to be anything you're not, it's just writing down this statement – which is a declaration of the "dream" level of confidence what you want to have. Turn that feeling into a statement.

For example, if you were in property development and wanted to feel successful, you might write:

Affirmative Statement: *"I am the number-one property developer on the West Coast, making a large income, winning awards and loving life."*

Right now, you may not believe a word of this statement – it's a sentence describing the career-confidence *you would like to have* if you could.

And now, underneath write down memories of all the times you've felt like that – or similar to that. You may well not have felt *that* confident, but I'm sure you've been close. It's less about the words you use and more about inhabiting the memory until you feel it just like you did when you got the compliment or were in that situation the first time. What you write isn't important – it's just a focal point to evoke the memory, which you then stay with for a few moments. Remember exactly how you felt. It's this feeling of confidence that is more important than what words you write. For example:

Affirmative Statement: *"I am the number-one property developer on the West Coast, making a large income, winning awards and loving life."*

- *Zach said I was going to be world-renowned, and I was amazing at what I do.*
- *When I sold the waterfront property, I felt like I was number one.*
- *My figures last year were the top five in the company.*
- *Lena said she always knew I'd be a huge success and be wealthy.*

As in the example above, you recall real-life events. For example, you might remember that time you were sitting in that restaurant with your ex-work colleague Joe. You were deep in conversation when he looked at you with certainty and said you were going to be a world-renowned property developer. Or the time you were in the office and Amit told you that you were in the top five in the company and you felt on top of the world. Or you had that great evening with Sara, took a walk on the beach, and she told you she always knew you'd be rich and successful.

You're not making anything up. You remember actual things that happened which made you feel how you'd imagine that Affirmative Statement would feel. Evoke at least 10 to 20 similar moments – take time with it. It's a really enjoyable practice to do once you get into it.

Confidence Evoke is about revisiting and remembering those times you felt confident and staying there for a few moments until you really feel it.

And remember, this isn't

complicated – it's a list of appreciation, remembering the "glass half full", that's all. You are not trying to pretend anything or make anything up: you are simply stating the facts. Through making this list, you'll realize that you are a lot closer to who and where you want to be than you think. You may even realize you're already there.

Repeat this technique until you own that Affirmative Statement; you claim it as your own. You can also do it on other subjects – it's particularly good for body confidence, and we will be returning to this technique in a later chapter.

- If there is something on your mind, apply the *"What's Good About…" List.*
- Use the *Freedom Process* to help you out with those areas where you're struggling to find the good in your *"What's Good About…" List.*
- Now you are clear, you can go straight into a gratitude list in the *Gratitude 150.*
- Use the *Confidence Evoke* for developing a consistently confident outlook and attitude by recalling those times when you felt successful.

WEEK 3

CONFIDENCE AND SELF-LOVE

When you step back, it's like you are your own angel – you are the person you've been asked to look after. But have you been doing that?

Continue with *Focal-point Meditation* and the *Higher Power List,* reminding yourself of the new practices by writing them on the left-hand side, for example, *Focal-point Meditation* (see page 40), *"What's Good About…" List* (see page 61), *Freedom Process* (see page 68) and *Confidence Evoke* (see page 77) – and perhaps your chosen form of physical exercise.

In the morning, if your mind is clear following meditation and there's nothing you are battling, you can go straight into *Confidence Evoke.* However, if there *is* something on your mind, face your feelings about the situation and the situation itself with the *"What's Good About…" List* and the *Freedom Process.*

This week you'll be focusing on you. Building on the techniques you learned in the previous weeks to increase confidence and self-love by recognizing the person within you – and putting you first. This is vital to be an empowered support for others, so it's not selfish in the way it might sound. Using this week's techniques, you'll learn how to turn the focus from your outward life and your reaction to it – to this person within you. These three tools are all about giving yourself what you are looking for someone else or an outer situation to give you. Giving that person time and space and unconditional support. It's a new way of developing self-confidence and self-love by acknowledging this person, to soothe feelings of abandonment or feelings of not enough.

> Techniques and tools are marked with 🕊 and are introduced over the four-week course. It's a good idea to find time for at least three practices a day but do what works best for you. At the end of the course, on page 119, you'll find a chart of all the tools and practices covered, which you can use to create your own personalized daily plan.

You Are Your Priority – and *Then* You Can Love Others

This is how most people live, unaware of the person within them – we feel invisible. Some people live for being kind to other people – which is great – but something is missing. You see, putting everyone else first all the time isn't always as loving as you may have thought – because it's putting *you* last all the time. *And you are a person too.*

Just as we so often end up seeking love and acceptance outside of ourselves, so too do we look for respect from other people or situations. But since respect isn't to be found out there, and the world mirrors back the level of respect you feel for yourself, you must make the first move. It's almost like one of our tasks is to be our own angel, guide or encourager – but we've forgotten this and looked to others to do it for us. It's like we ignore ourselves, and instead, give attention to others. This self-abandonment is the source of a lot of disconnection.

Discover the Person Within and Empower Yourself

🕊 *Self-realization Process*

Your eyes are the way you receive information – and you connect at a deeper level with other people by looking directly into their eyes when you speak to them. Connecting with *your* eyes, you'll discover that you are a person and as such *you* are the support you have been looking for, accessible in every moment through a mirror or similar reflective surface. This is a great way to use a mirror – as a place to drop yourself a nice feeling or two, encouraging the person you see there.

The term "self-realization" has many meanings in spiritual terms – but in this context, it's about connecting with your inner Self and recognizing that you are a person to be loved. It is about realizing that *you* are a person and in the mirror is the most powerful champion of you that you will ever find. So now you want to begin deliberately using a mirror to relate with that person inside of you: that person you are. That sometimes-isolated person within deserves love – and this process is a powerful and clear way to give yourself love and acceptance. Then, this love and acceptance will mirror outward into your life. Also, you will find the more you love yourself, the less likely you will go into intense dwelling on thoughts – which simply doesn't feel good and isn't self-loving.

The more you care for that person within, the more you will naturally choose to focus on love rather than overthinking.

How to Do the *Self-realization Process*

For some people, looking in the mirror is a miserable experience that just reminds them of what's wrong with the way they look. And that is why it's vital that you only use this technique when you are already feeling OK, and you already have a good grounding in the practices I've shared in the previous weeks. If not, the temptation to look at your physical body and critique it (even though that's not what this process is) may be too strong. And, if you look in the mirror when you don't feel good, the mirror simply reflects back your mood, and you will probably not like what you see and go into overthinking about your body image (see chapter on "Looking and Feeling Your Best Self" for more on this). But if you're ready, here's how to use the process.

1. Find a mirror.
2. Look at yourself deeply in the eyes. Your focus may go to your face and start to analyse your features etc. – but come back to your eyes and know that "I am on your side. I am here for you".
3. Stay with your eyes. All the time let your thoughts drift away like clouds. Wait for a connection to happen between you and your eyes – it's just you and the eyes.
4. Breathe deeply and slowly. Wait for the love to come flooding from within you toward the person in the mirror and from the person in the mirror to you, like waiting for a Wi-Fi connection to connect-in.
5. Apologize to yourself for abandoning yourself and feel the apology coming back to you.
6. Tell yourself you are beautiful and feel the appreciation come back from the reflection to you.
7. Offer yourself a "thank you" for the amazing person you are – and feel thanked and loved in return.

When you recall those teachers who had a great effect on you from school, and when you read about superstars talking about those people who changed their life, you find the greatest mentors say the same kind of thing. They don't try to fix or correct. They just see your truth – your talent. They are amazed by you and say, "You can do it, you are on track. You're amazing." Be that mentor for yourself. See that person in the mirror as your champion ready to uplift you.

In every mirror you happen to walk past or deliberately get up in front of, you've got a meeting with a powerful supporter there waiting to cheer you on. Make use of it. Walking to work, you could drop yourself a compliment as you notice your reflection in the windows of a building – speak it quietly to yourself. In these brief moments you get with one another (you and your inner Self), use this time well – and go for it. Just one sentiment or sentence will do. Connect with your eyes and communicate a reassuring feeling. Give that person you see a compliment. Give yourself what you are looking for out there from other people. Feel that love of your Higher Power enveloping you.

When you're at home, if you feel you need attention – look in a mirror and tell yourself what you are waiting for other people to tell you (which is a variation of "you are loved, and you are perfect just as you are") – it will be a whole new level for you. As you are loving to your Self, life mirrors this back.

Some people get very complicated with their mirror techniques, but I teach just this one: Connect with your eyes and feel love for that person. And that's enough.

Over the years, many teachings have explored using your reflection to help yourself feel better – but I've spoken to more than a few people who said that this made them feel worse. And that's because they didn't discover the most important step of all. As I suggested, when you make contact with a mirror, the first thing your lower-self mind/overthinking personality will do is critique your appearance. It doesn't matter who you are – it will zoom in and start criticizing. Learning to admire your body in the mirror might be a great thing to do some other time – but that is not this process. This technique is not about looking at the body – it's about connecting to that person behind your eyes.

Another Way to Do the *Self-realization Process*

When the tendency to critique your body is too much, you can also do the *Self-realization Process* with your eyes closed instead. This practice also works very well if you can't sleep: just hold yourself in your mind's eye as you drift off to sleep. No one knows you like you – and you know exactly how to treat yourself with love.

1. Lie down in bed or sit in a comfortable chair and close your eyes.
2. In your mind's eye, see yourself standing next to the person you know as you, looking back on yourself, as if you are a

friend of yours, looking at this person that is you. You are seeing the person you've been asked to look after – but have you been looking after you?

3. See yourself receiving a loving hug. No words are necessary, just hold yourself – in your imagination – and relax. You don't have to strive for this love or earn this love – you are loved, just as you are.

Someone who attended one of my groups shared that she closes her eyes and holds herself in her mind's eye while she has a bath, and she said it made the bath feel even more nurturing as she connected with herself. Now, she looks forward to her "bath process" as she calls it – and always feels bathed in love for self when she finishes, refreshed and revitalized and ready for the day (or evening) ahead.

Be a Good Friend to Yourself

It is important to become a good friend to yourself. Someone I coached said he had put a little desk mirror on its side between his double bed pillows to give himself comfort when going through a breakup. He lay down, and it seemed like he was lying in bed next to himself. No abandonment occurred because he had himself to comfort himself through it all! He started to see that other person as a partner he lived with. His loneliness melted away, and he started feeling confident about himself and his life.

All this being your own champion and companion initially sounds sad or even cringe-worthy – but it's transformational. And it makes you very attractive indeed – in all ways. If you can be kind to that person you are, this will create confidence – and this vibe will go outward, and you will be irresistible and incredibly in-demand. There will be "something about you". I know a guy who did this, and he credits this process to "randomly" getting scouted on the street and is now a hugely popular model.

People who feel ignored or unappreciated forget that it is predominantly them who is ignoring themselves, not realizing their own value and not appreciating themselves. This technique will change all that. Give yourself the appreciation and the validation you were looking to others for. The power we have is when we decide to give ourselves what we are most looking for.

> The *Self-realization Process* is about realizing that you too are a person to give love to.

Someone came to me and said she believes what you give out you get back. She was so kind to people and yet one person was bullying her. I asked her, how do you speak to/treat yourself? It suddenly clicked. She realized how unkind she was to herself, in her own inner dialogue. She had forgotten she was a person and so, through the *Self-realization Process*, she realized that she could use what was happening to stop bullying herself (not to excuse the person bullying her) and as an invitation to love herself more.

Asking the Person Within You What *They* Want

If you're unsure about whether to get involved in a certain relationship or behavioural choice, step out of yourself and look back at the person within you. And ask yourself: "Is it loving to take [*insert your own name here*] to this place?" See yourself as separate to you, pause – and listen for the answer and ask yourself. For example, "What would be the best way to treat [*insert your own name here*] right now? To tuck [*insert your own name here*] up in bed right now, for example? To order an amazing meal for [*insert your own name*] or to buy [*insert your own name*] an amazing outfit?"

When you are considering a choice, ask yourself: "Is this a self-loving thing to do?"

Ask yourself: "Would I take [*insert your name here*] into this situation and introduce them to this person?" Is it self-respecting to interact with that person or spend time with them? Would you take someone you loved there? Ask the question "Is it loving for you?" and "Is it loving for them?" Is it loving? And then feel for the answer.

Take Back Your Power

Magic Button

This technique is a quick way of stopping those manic and panicky thoughts, which sometimes come from feeling out of control in a situation and being dependent on other's behaviour. It's about taking your power back. Start by writing down the thing you *think* you want to happen that's stopping you from feeling good right now. Let me show you how the technique works by giving an example: You think you want a certain person to call you and tell you that you are special and that they love and appreciate you. For example:

Mark calls me and tells me I'm good looking, magnetic and an amazing person, and he wants to see me all the time.

You sit there, and it's not happening. He's not calling you. He doesn't seem bothered. You feel a sinking feeling; your thoughts go into overdrive, and you're feeling not good enough, not attractive enough, etc. and then you really need him to call you. *And he's not calling you.*

So, you get a piece of paper and write down these words: "Mark calls me and tells me I'm good looking, magnetic and an amazing person, and he wants to see me all the time."

Then draw a line underneath those words. This is what you want to happen if you could push a button and make it happen. Underneath write the words, "I want to feel…"

Now list how you imagine you would feel if Mark was to call you and tell you those words: that he finds you incredibly good looking, magnetic, an amazing person, he wants to see you all the time and so on. Write how you would feel if Mark told you he was totally in love with you and you are his ideal partner. Keep writing the words "I want to feel…" line-by-line, adding new feelings as you go along. For example:

- *I want to feel attractive.*
- *I want to feel respected.*
- *I want to feel acknowledged.*
- *I want to feel adored.*

Keep on going down the page, writing the feelings you'd feel if this happened.

- *I want to feel good about myself.*
- *I want to feel gorgeous.*
- *I want to feel eligible.*
- *I want to feel secure.*
- *I want to feel loved.*
- *I want to feel honoured and special.*
- *I want to feel like God's gift.*
- *I want to feel free.*

Keep writing, keep on identifying more and more feelings. Remember, you're not trying to feel these feelings – you are just trying to identify the feelings you think you want to feel, and you would feel if what you wanted actually happened.

When you're finished, answer these questions:

1. If this situation happened (Mark calling and telling you that you're amazing, etc.), can you absolutely, 100 per cent, be sure that you'd feel these feelings consistently?
2. And, if you had a choice, would you want the situation to happen (Mark calling and telling you that you're amazing, etc.)? Or, would you want to consistently feel and embody the "I want to feel…" list of feelings you wrote?

Getting What You Really Want

The list of feelings you wrote down shows you what you really want. You think if you get what you want (in this case, Mark calling), you'd feel all these feelings… and you might – but probably not for long, as you've probably felt this way before about another part of life. In other words, you have a weak muscle on this subject where you are prone to emotionally collapsing into victim-overthinking.

You see, if we have a weak muscle in our self-worth, we will choose someone like Mark who won't be into us. Or Mark will be into us, but at times he won't be – when we're feeling needy, for example – because we want to see where we have weak muscles. We have no idea what's going on in Mark's life, but we can be sure we will have him mirror us in some way.

It's not that *they* are not bothered about us, but *we* are not bothered about us – "they" are simply holding up a mirror to what we believe. This is why when you are feeling empowered and loving yourself, then you light up – and they are into you.

So, when someone you like doesn't call you back or seems disinterested, do you collapse into low self-worth – or do you feel that perhaps they weren't a match for your greatness?

In the first example, you might resent the other person, because you've taken their decision to be all about your value – when it never is. In the second, you can swiftly let go and move on – and even wish them well. But the other person hasn't done anything differently – it's all about your opinion of you. Take responsibility for your level of self-worth. If you felt eligible right now, you would feel alright. And so, this situation is only about one thing: an opportunity to train into unshakeable self-confidence or self-love, just like you wanted to. Leave the other person out of it – they are not the point of this, *you* are. The other person's behaviour is showing you what you are not giving yourself – and is a nudge for you to give more of that quality to yourself.

This process is best used in situations when you feel you've given away your power, or you feel that someone, or something, has to change before you can feel good. For example, you might use this process with difficult relationships – such as a friend you've fallen out with, conflict with your parents, a bullying work colleague or boss – or anyone who's behaving differently than the way you think they should. You can also use this process for situations, such as not getting the job you want or something going differently to the way you wanted it to go. People spend a lifetime trying to manipulate others to make the right behaviour happen. Sometimes it works, temporarily; often it doesn't. But it isn't enough to make you consistently feel good – and the *Magic Button* wakes you up to see that this situation has alerted you to where you need to love yourself more. If you could feel the feeling, you'd have what you want without anything else needing to change and then life mirrors all of that back to you.

Dealing with Intense, Difficult Relationship Emotions

Relationship Trigger

The *Relationship Trigger* is the most powerful technique I've yet found for dealing with the high emotions that tend to come up in romantic relationships "gone-wrong". It's something you can do in the moment of those emotional storms, and often provides instant soothing. With practice, you will be a lot more confident going into relationships – as you know, you can deal with whatever comes up.

Like many people I used to be scared of the feelings that came up when a relationship ended: feelings which left me feeling insecure within relationships, worried about what I'd do if it "went wrong". Some people feel terrible when a partner does something they weren't expecting, like being dishonest or even taking a step back from the relationship. These feelings of disappointment or abandonment can be intense. Most of the bestselling music out there is about this feeling (love songs are rarely about love) – and so it's nothing to be ashamed of. It's just one of those feelings that we don't like admitting, so you can feel like it's just you going through it. For a long time, I couldn't work out why "relationship stuff" seemed so intense compared to other subjects.

If you're in this situation, first remind yourself it's OK to feel awful when you've been shunned or ignored by someone – particularly if they don't or won't tell you why. It's a strength to feel these feelings – it shows you are genuine and you care and you are in a better place than you know. You want to ask (as in almost a prayer, on the *Higher Power List*) for stamina and endurance. Don't shy away from feelings or pain – all great journeys have intense sensation within them. So, see yourself handing over this pain and tangle of emotions to your Real Self (or a name for a Higher Power) to oversee the situation. Imagine an elixir pouring into your solar plexus and strengthening it.

Sometimes the painful feelings are about someone you just started dating who suddenly stops calling you back. If this is the case, you may tell yourself that you haven't known them for long and therefore "you shouldn't feel devastated and you're being dramatic" – but this response is still in the area of self-attack. Your feelings are OK; you want to embrace your reaction and embrace yourself.

> It's OK to feel as I feel. It's OK to react as I react.

It's Not About Them

When those hopeless feelings come up, it can seem serious, like the world is ending. This can work like drug withdrawal, and the confusion happens when we think that we then really *need* that person back to be happy. This is a trick. The compelling feeling you feel – the feeling of abandonment and the need for them – is not a call for them but a call for you. It's part of *you* calling out to be embraced. It's a call for self-love. That is why this feeling moves from person to person. This feeling of abandonment is nothing to do with the current relationship or that person at all, despite how much it can seem like it is. It's just a nudge to love yourself more.

> What happens is people feel a painful trigger and then blame someone else for it. We include someone else in the mix. When really, it's between you and the trigger.

How to Use the *Relationship Trigger*

You've just been triggered by a relationship. You feel overwhelmed by it. You have that feeling in the pit of your stomach or chest area, you can't focus, and you feel like the rug's been pulled from under you. Now is the time to do this process.

1. Get to a safe space where you can close your eyes. Grab a pillow or cushion or even a soft toy.
2. Hold the pillow against where you are feeling the anxiety – this itself will provide relief.
3. Imagine this cushion is your inner child Self, who wants to be loved and held. Remember to breathe deeply in and out as you hold this child – this version of you. You are holding "you" until you feel relief. If you find your mind trying to run away with your thoughts, just come back to holding the child within. Come back to the person within you. Comfort this person. Give yourself – that person – your *undivided attention.*
4. Every time you think of the person or people who are the reason for you doing this process – those people that don't make you feel good – just throw an imaginary blanket over them and come back to giving yourself undivided attention. It's OK to feel as you feel. Turn your back on those other people or stories and embrace the child within. *You're abandoning yourself by going into stories about them – instead, choose you.*
5. Notice how the mind wants to go outside and go into stories about "them" (the other person). But this is about you. This is about holding yourself and leaving all the stories about the world aside. Leave the stories out of it, cover them with the blanket of clouds and just hold yourself – words aren't necessary.
6. Keep doing this process until you feel soothed back into your Real Self. Once you feel relief, which could take a few minutes or longer, the process is done, and you can get up and go on with your day.

Remember, this process is not about other people. Your attention may go to them, and the stories about them will keep starting up. But come back to the breath. In your mind's eye, throw a blanket over them and the situation. Keep on throwing a blanket over them, over your shoulder, so to speak, while

Keep on reminding yourself to stay within. Stay holding that child within. This love is your shield.

you're giving yourself undivided attention and love.

The source of your pain is when you abandon yourself. This situation that triggered you is a gift: the situation didn't cause the pain, it just triggered something that was already there. It's abandoning ourselves that causes the pain; it's got nothing to do with them or "the situation". All relationship pain is this, although people think it's because the other person abandoned them.

You'll find the more you do this process, the easier it will be and it will strengthen your self-love. Next time you feel relationship anxiety, you will instantly see it as a call from your inner child to love your inner child – it's your time to be a guardian to that child. And now, you will leave everyone else out of it. In this way, you will become empowered, free and not "needy" at all. Fewer things will happen to you which cause these feelings to begin with, and so you won't need to do this process so much. You'll realize these experiences of abandonment were only happening anyway to "wake you up" to the fact that you were abandoning yourself. Once you give yourself the love that you need, the situations you encounter out there in the mirror of life will be more naturally loving and respectful.

- Use the *Magic Button* to show yourself what you really want is a feeling – not someone to change.
- Acknowledge and recognize the incredible person within you with the *Self-realization Process*.
- Soothe and clear any patterns of abandonment using the *Relationship Trigger*. Every time you feel that powerless feeling of abandonment, give yourself the unconditional support that you are looking to the other person to give you.

WEEK 4
BE MORE YOU

When you are yourself, you have no competition, you find your path and your people – and life works. Being yourself crowds overthinking out of your mind and keeps you in that empowered, confident space.

By this point, you have all the tools you need to clear your mind, develop self-appreciation and confidence. It takes time to get good at this, so be patient and gentle with yourself as you are learning this new approach. Remember, it's OK not to be centred, and to go into overthinking, and not always accept where you are. It's better than OK – it's a workout.

If you've made peace, you've let go, you feel clear-minded – you've been doing the previous techniques daily – then it's time to move to these final techniques, so you don't get stuck in the past or go back to old habits of overthinking. The lower-self mind likes to think – that's what keeps it going – and if you find that you've made peace but still want to go back, it's probably the lower-self mind wanting to dwell in thoughts.

Your mind may want to keep going back and thinking of the problem in the guise of making peace – but you have already made peace with it.

The *Higher Power List* from Week 1 (see page 36) works well if you are feeling overwhelmed. But if you're feeling clear-minded, you may want to discontinue this as a daily practice unless you are guided to. But don't abandon everything that's come before. When you have given your power away, call it back with the *Magic Button* (see page 88) and the *Relationship Trigger* (see page 91). And remember to love who you are, coaching yourself as you encounter a reflection of yourself throughout your day through the *Self-realization Process* (see page 82).

Gratitude (which includes the *"What's Good About..." List*, see page 61, and *Confidence Evoke*, see page 77) and *Focal-point Meditation* (see page 40) can be like "leg day" at the gym – not something you particularly want to do, and sometimes you want to avoid it – but vital for getting the complete results you want. What I'm saying is, keep doing these "foundational" practices – and also move forward to these next techniques.

The week is all about maintaining the confidence you have been developing in the previous weeks. You are now clear-minded and ready to go to the next level. The first practice, *FreeSelf Anchors (Declarations),* keeps you anchored in your confidence and prevents all that nonsense mind chatter coming back in. Then we move onto a way to deal with those desires for things that you haven't got or that aren't happening with the *Retrospective Process*. Finally, we move to the *Starboard*, which is a visual reminder of what you love about life and how to live life to the max.

> Techniques and tools are marked with 🕊 and are introduced over the four-week course. It's a good idea to find time for at least three practices a day but do what works best for you. At the end of the course, on page 119, you'll find a chart of all the tools and practices covered, which you can use to create your own personalized daily plan.

Stay Centred and Assume the Power

🕊 *FreeSelf Anchors (Declarations)*

As you leave your meditation and your written techniques and walk out into your day, you may notice that your mind is prone to veering off into mind chatter. Eventually, the mind chatter is going to get your attention. And although it may not be as intense as it was before – and you have the tools to deal with it this time – there is a better way.

Although it may be difficult to control your thoughts, the words you speak *can* be controlled more easily – and this practice is about deliberately using your words. Repeating words you speak in your mind are a good way to hold your attention and prevent mind-wandering, especially when you are out and about, and it's not possible to do *Focal-point Meditation* (which requires closed eyes). The words are an anchor; something solid to take hold of and provide a focal point sometimes more tangible than focusing on your breath or an image or a sound.

Often people confuse saying words with thinking, but they are totally different. Speaking words aloud (or aloud in your mind) is like a snow plough that pushes through the snowstorm of thoughts. As with many of the techniques I've shared so far, it's about focusing on something other than your thoughts and *FreeSelf Anchors (Declarations)* is no different. It's so easy to just go into thoughts – it can take a bit of effort to choose instead to speak words. It's about choosing to speak words over choosing to think thoughts and allowing them to hold your attention and prevent your mind wandering into thoughts.

How to Use *FreeSelf Anchors (Declarations)*

Before you begin, choose your declaration – the statement you will take into your day, and repeat over and over throughout the day when your mind is at risk of wandering into negative mind chatter. It doesn't really matter what you choose for your phrase, but you want to make sure it is relaxing and empowering– something you can just repeat over and over without thinking about it too much. We are all different, and that's why you want to find this phrase for yourself.

> It's not about the words but more about the focus the words give you.

One way of coming up with a phrase is this: Choose a noun – you could choose "man" or "woman" or "person" – any word which you feel comfortable in describing you. Then find adjectives and add them on. Make your declaration in the present tense, for example: "I am a beautiful, strong, connected, powerful, loved, successful, loving, wealthy, magnetic person." Keep on going, finding verbs to put in front of your selected noun. "I am a successful, dynamic, attractive, beautiful, strong, powerful, sexy, wealthy, happy, blessed, loved, loving, happy, confident man/woman."

Some people like a shorter sentence as it's easier to remember, and others like something longer and more complex so that they really have to focus on repeating it; to powerfully hold their mind and prevent it wandering into thoughts. Just go with what feels right for you. This is your statement or declaration. Get creative and see what words flow, create your own.

For example:

"I love my great life – I am happy and free. Life is on my side. I am limitless, and blessings are all around me – all is good in my life. I bless everyone I meet, and my life is incredible. Thank you for the blessings for myself and my loved ones. I am loved and adored and blessed – all my loved ones are loved and adored and blessed."

"I am strong, confident and attractive. Everything I'm involved with is a success. All the situations in my life come into balance, and everyone around me finds their way and is empowered, happy and successful."

Sometimes people ask me to help them come up with a statement, but it's important to create your own and use ideas that "click" with you. Be spontaneous and creative. Write your own script – and then repeat it until you remember it and take it into your day.

Declarations hold you in your centre; they are FreeSelf Anchors.

Declarations are not about trying to think or battling to be something you're not (which will get you into thoughts). So, you might not want to use "I am attractive and beautiful" if you've got an intense problem with body image at the moment. If what's on your mind is lack of money – you may want to drop the word "wealthy" from your list, as this may get you to attempt to overthink it. If you're feeling really insecure, leave out "confident", for now. Choosing declarations around areas that are seriously bothering you *right in this moment* may be difficult.

Declarations are about using a point of focus (words) to hold your attention to *prevent* your mind from wandering into thoughts, not to get you to think more. They're about keeping you anchored in that "superconscious" lane. And so, when you choose your declarations, make sure they are something that you already know is true – or at least something you know you don't disbelieve. In the way, your thoughts will not argue with the statement you are speaking. For example, you already know you are a talented artist, so you can use "I am a talented artist". Or you already know you have the potential to be a successful actor, and in many ways, you are doing that for your job: "I am a successful actor" would work to be your declaration. Bring in words that describe your *current* career or life: "I am a bestselling artist, successful, loved, popular, etc." The key is don't add anything you don't really believe you are or something you feel needy about. It is all about declaring what you know to be true, and what feels easy and exciting for you right now.

The key is to repeat this phrase over and over, until you feel securely anchored in a confident state of mind. It's harder than it sounds, at least initially. As with many of these practices, the beginning is the time the mind chatter will talk you out of it with "what's the point of this, what a waste of my mind" or "this won't work" or "this is boring", but continue through that. What's the alternative? To think all that nonsense mind chatter, where has that got you? All this opposition and doubt is just mind chatter which is in the way of what you want. So, stick to the declaration

> Just like a speaker broadcasting an important message – this is not about emotion or thinking – it's just about confidently speaking out the words. Take declarations seriously – and go for it, over and over.

anyway and keep on going as it elevates you above thought. Behind the mind chatter are all the new insights and ideas you are looking for – so it's not like declarations will put you in a state of blankness. In fact, many people have told me that really good ideas start coming to them when they clear their mind with declarations.

You Are Already There... Now What?

Retrospective Process

It might now look as if the course is shifting focus by looking to create a better life in the future rather than enjoying our life today – but it only looks that way. Visualization is all about making the most of Now; it is another process to enjoy the present moment.

Conventional visualization techniques usually ask us to imagine our life just as we want it to be and tell us that if we replay these images often enough, then they will manifest. It's not so much that I disagree with the theory, but in practice, it often doesn't work so well. I've met very few people who have been able to live in the vision as if it's real, consistently, because making that shift into envisioning your dreams as if they're real can plunge us into doubt and disbelief. If that sounds like you, you're not alone. Surprisingly if you read into the biographies of some of those famed teachers of visualization – it didn't work so successfully for them either. They found it more difficult than it appeared to be, too.

The problem is visualization so often keeps us out of the present moment and in overthinking. And "faking it until you make it" becomes like a continuous game of fancy dress or "let's pretend". You know it isn't real – and so does life. Instead, you need to let loose of your ambitions and desires for the future before you can authentically appreciate your

> Successful visualization is about making the most of Now; it is another process to enjoy the present moment.

current life. Enter the *Retrospective Process,* which will help you to disengage from your desires so you can get on with loving your life. It doesn't disempower your desires but puts them in their place, leaving you free to enjoy the present moment, which is key to living your best life.

How to Use the *Retrospective Process*

We all have a list of "I'll be happy when..." but it often prevents us from experiencing the great potential of today, and every day. With this attitude, all you get mirrored back is a constant feeling of waiting for your life to happen. Even knowing this, we still have our list of "I'll be happy when's". That's OK, the *Retrospective Process* shows you what to do with that list.

Get a piece of paper and draw a horizontal line midway across the page. In the space above the line, write a list of all those things that you really want to happen; your list of "I'll be happy when's...." It could be your dream relationship, enough cash in the bank, or your ideal body. Whatever comes to mind. Whatever you desire – and that means all of them – that is stopping you being fully complete in this moment. It's like some Higher Power is saying to you "What can I give that will help you fully enjoy your life today?" Write down everything that if you had it, you could relax.

Ask yourself: "What is it that I want? What do I need to happen so I can fully enjoy today?" Don't hold back and write everything down.

Keep on writing down those things that come to mind; things that you can't figure out how they could happen today. Every time you think of something you want – which you'll unlikely have today (and is, therefore, stopping you fully making the most of today) – just write it down above the line. Spend a few moments going into the feeling of each one as if it were accomplished, and then move on to the next.

Stay with the list. Add some more detail to each point. You're not writing them down because some Higher Power needs the detail – it's for you. You can relax knowing that they are being taken care of; you feel *answered;* you feel *heard.* Write things for other people too – to soothe those fears about other people that may be stopping you fully enjoying your present moment. For example:

- *Fully booked waiting list – number one at what I do.*
- *Enough money for two houses.*
- *Magazine features agreed and planned.*
- *Amazing friendships and relationships.*
- *Warehouse apartment, city centre – contract signed.*
- *New camera.*
- *Jada has a great trip and her relationship is sorted.*
- *Maserati ordered.*
- *Stephanie is in perfect health and is enjoying life.*
- *Amazing relationship with my soulmate.*
- *Furniture for flat.*
- *Toned/muscled body.*

This list of things that you want is the reason that you are doing most of the things you are doing; they are what you spend much of the day overthinking about. You are not doing most of the things that you do for enjoyment – but in an attempt to achieve this list. Your life revolves around achieving this list. And it's not working to achieve the list, the things on it always seem to be a step away. This also takes up a huge amount of your time, thinking about what you want and how you plan to achieve it – time that you are going to have freed up. So, keep on writing the list. Anything you want to be different or you need or want, or that comes to mind that is in the way of you fully enjoying today put above the line.

The *Retrospective Process* is about fast-forwarding to that step beyond your dream and then looking back.

Now move to the lower half of the page and write a heading: "Now what?"

Ask yourself: "What would I do today if I had accomplished what I wanted?"

This is your things-to-do-now list, assuming you already have what you've just written down. You may have to sit awhile and wait for ideas to come in. If you had what you wanted, you wouldn't just sit there forever, popping champagne corks. There is a life to be lived!

Let's say you are *already* that famous actor with the film on at the cinema, or an in-demand barber with a fully booked waiting list or whatever it is you do. You've got that bodybuilding champion's body. *Now, what are you going to do today?*

Write the words "Now what?" and underline them, and then list each task in turn. Taking action is the declaration and immediately brings you to that feeling of already being that which you want to be. For example:

- *Paint.*
- *Get food in plus the coffee at that new popular café.*
- *Get a haircut.*
- *Order the magazine subscription.*
- *Get a new notebook – the make/type I want.*
- *Gratitude 150.*
- *Focal-point Meditation.*
- *Be totally myself – wear my new suit.*

Some people put off going to a particular restaurant or dressing the way they want purely because they think they must wait for their dreams to come true before they can do it. Putting off life, allowing ambition to block enjoying today, also potentially blocks their success. Once you put above the line what you define as "making it", and write what you can do on your "Now what?" list, you do what it is you want to do, *today*. Yes, you may be out of your comfort zone – but do it anyway. Of course, if there's anything on your "Now what?" list that is too expensive for your right now, or out of

Every time you think of something that is beyond your means today – add it "above the line".

your reach in some way, write it above the line (maxing out on credit cards is not what I'm encouraging at all). In the example, I've written that the car is "ordered" or the property is "signed for", so interacting with it isn't an option today. You can't put "drive new car" or "go to new property" on your "Now what?" list – you want it to involve a different action to what you wrote above the line. So assume you have got what you want, and then do something unrelated – something you would do once the excitement of having it settled down. So you might have your car on order, and on your "Now what?" list you could go for a walk, or go to a local café.

When you remove the blocks of your desires, you get to see your life, sometimes for the first time. You get to be *you.* Using this process, you will become much happier and contented – and in-sync with your Real Self, which deep down is what many of us are searching for anyway. Now you are going to focus on even more ideas for the "Now what?" part of the *Retrospective Process*. It's time to start enjoying your life as you even more. It's interesting and amazing how many people are not being them in life; they end up missing out on a great deal of life. You are going to discover what you really enjoy in life and how you want to spend your time. When you feel that enthusiasm, your life experience upgrades to a whole new level.

Being Yourself Fully
Starboard

Being more you is the success secret you are looking for.

If you got all the people you call successful in a room and lined them up, you'd see they were all different heights and shapes and sizes with different looks and different personalities. Some would talk a lot and be the life and soul of the party. Others would be quieter and more reserved. You'd end up not knowing what the one thing that brought them all together in that category of "successful" was. If you asked them, they would probably each tell you their own totally different methods or "steps" that were their secret to success.

But there is one thing they all do have in common: *they are being more them than the competition is being them.* That's what makes them memorable and unforgettable. It's not that they are working harder than everyone else – if that were the case, they'd retire with all that wealth once they'd created it.

They are successful due to being themselves – which is surely everyone's dream job. They are literally being paid for being them.

So it's not about improving yourself or personally developing yourself or creating a different life. It is about being you, now – without any additions or fixing. It's standing tall as you. Being yourself *now* is what you are looking for. Not doing this or that to be ready… "and then I'll be me." It sounds so easy – "just be you". So why isn't it?

The *Starboard* stops you worrying about what other people think of you.

Caring What People Think

What holds us back from being fully ourselves is usually the opposite of being more yourself – the fear of what people will think. Being fully yourself fills the space where thought once was. Being yourself is a big, expressive experience that takes up room. This doesn't necessarily mean you are externally loud or expressive – in fact, some people who are being fully themselves have a cool, calm demeanour. However, your inner space is filled with "you" like a balloon which has been inflated to the max, leaving no space for the lower-self mind and its thoughts. You are not thinking, you are being – there's no room left for thinking. Being yourself keeps you out of thought and clears your mind. This is why this practice, the *Starboard*, asks you to focus on things that excite you, to prevent that mind wandering into thoughts such as "what will they think".

Finding Your "Stars" for Your *Starboard*

Those dynamic interests that you recorded on your *Higher Power List* in Week 1 will have arrived as ideas that "just came to you". You may already have started these new hobbies or projects. Dramas and problems attempt to get your attention – but it is your interest in them that keeps you stuck in the storm clouds of thinking. The *Starboard* is a reminder of those things that get you excited – more excited than the dramas and problems.

By this stage, if you've been using the practices consistently, you'll be feeling a lot more clear-minded. At this stage, it's often light-hearted pastimes that keep you in your flow. Like the multi-millionaire businessman I knew, who said his secret to success was collecting memorabilia from his favourite TV series, *Star Trek*. He spent hours searching for a rare or "one-off" piece to add to his collection, and it stopped him going into mind chatter. It was his meditation. In the whole process of finding the latest figure or model spaceship or original comic or whatever, he came up with the most amazing ideas for his business; they just came to him. Now I'm not saying you have to collect *Star Trek* memorabilia. That was *his* "thing". But you certainly want to find "your thing".

So after you've anchored your mind, you want to move your focus on to that thing that excites you and gets you up out of bed, be it a mission, a cause, fashion, collecting things, sports, a dream career – whatever it is. I like to call these things "stars". The *Starboard* is an "artboard", where you creatively write a list of all these things that you love, and then you put it on your wall to remind yourself. It's a nudge to do active appreciation. When you are doing something that you love with focus, you are living in appreciation. You are taking your "attitude of gratitude" out into the day. Having meaning and purpose is the next level to fill the "vacuum" that releasing overthinking has left.

Find that thing that gets you leaping out of bed in the morning and do it.

A star is an ignition: it's a firelighter; it's a spark of excitement that takes you into your day flying high above thoughts, onto that superhighway "winning" lane, where the best of life happens. You want to find those dynamic stars to focus on: something that excites you – and excites you more than your problems do. Choose stars which have to do with your life purpose or mission – and ideas for actions will come to you, which you can then engage with in the perfect time. And so, your morning routine of sweeping thoughts aside passes the baton to these actions, and so being your Real Self more consistently through the day is possible. The party, the exciting event, is where *you* are. The *Starboard* will remind you of that.

Creating Your *Starboard*

For this technique, you'll need a piece of paper or card – A4 or larger. You'll also need a pen or preferably pens in different styles or colours. Unlike the other practices, the *Starboard* is more of a one-off thing you do, like creating a piece of art. You create it and then display it. You can, also, add to it every now and then, though.

1. Turn the paper, so it is landscape.
2. Now pause and wait and see what comes to mind first. You are looking for your stars – which means subjects, interests and ideas that excite you.
3. Once you've decided on your five to ten stars, write each one on the page – space out the words around the page, perhaps in circles or clouds. Write a star next to each word or sentence. Doodle pictures next to the words if you want, and imagine this as your piece of art. It doesn't matter if you see yourself as an artist or not but get creative. Write down the ideas that thrill you and get you to be more you.

Your *Starboard* reminds you of the purpose, meaning and excitement in your life.

The *Starboard* is not for writing things you long for – it's for things that excite you. It is a free-flying and an easy-going experience which will keep you engaged with life and feeling sky-high. I've never heard of anyone who created an amazing life by just sitting there and wishing – because that gets boring fast. You need something more dynamic, and this board will prompt you into action – it's a note-on-the-wall reminder of those things that you love to involve yourself with. Find those stars that represent ideas to get excited about.

Revel in being your Real Self.

Be artistic with your *Starboard*. Add colour, draw on it, make it attractive. And then put it on your wall or in your office. Create mini versions in different sizes. I know someone, an artist, who turned her *Starboard* into a full-on watercolour and then got

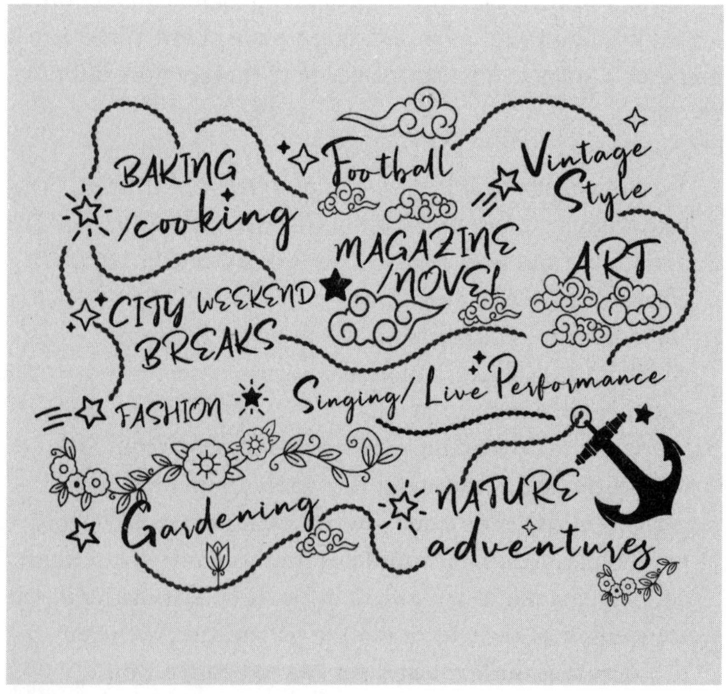

Figure 1. An example of a Starboard

business cards printed of the image. She didn't give these cards to anyone, she just put these mini works of art in drawers and cupboards all around her home to surprise herself later – to cheer herself up when she needed it, or remind her of what she was about in life. You may want to do the same – you don't have to get them printed, but you could create *Starboards* on blank business card-sized paper or card. Put these versions around your home, which you will see every now and then, and it will remind you of what makes you happy.

When you revel in being you and feel totally fulfilled in the moment, you are in that Real Self mode, and life will mirror back the best it has to offer, fit for a prince or princess. Get so much into being you that there is no room for doubt or other forms of mind chatter. Crowd out all of that chatter by being brighter, bigger and more fully your Real Self.

Tether your mind by focusing on a star from your *Starboard* or repeating those *FreeSelf Anchors (Declarations)* as you go. If you think this is somehow pointless or repetitive: how pointless or repetitive is mind chatter that just sets out to criticize yourself or others? Walk tall, whether you feel like it or not. Hold your poise. Stand tall and walk on, clear-minded. Dominate the space with being you. Own the space with being you. Crowd out all thoughts of "what will they think" by *being more you.*

- Use *FreeSelf Anchors (Declarations)* to prevent your mind wandering into thoughts.
- Deal with all those unfulfilled dreams and desires and make the most of your life today with the *Retrospective Process.*
- Remind yourself of those interests that excite you and get you leaping out of bed in the morning with the *Starboard.*

AFTER THE COURSE

QUESTIONS AND SOLUTIONS

It is doing the course rather than reading about it that's going to give you the results.

Keep on with the *Higher Power List* and *Focal-point Meditation* and, when you need to, use the *"What's Good About…" List* and the *Freedom Process* to get you centred. Then you can continue with either the *Confidence Evoke* or a straightforward list of appreciation or gratitude. When you are out and about, walking around and on the go and not able to do written work or "sit down" meditation, practices to use include the *FreeSelf Anchors (Declarations)* and the *Icon Switch*. Integrate any desires and goals with the *Retrospective Process*, which will shift you into that perspective of already living your ideal life, today. Have fun creating your *Starboard* and then get on with some of the activities on it. The *Starboard* will remind you of what you love to do; what things get you excited and loving life.

At the end of this chapter, on page 119, you'll find a chart and handy page reference guide to all the tools and practices covered in the four-week course, which you can use to create your own personalized daily plan.

I always enjoy hearing how much better people feel when they get "out of their own way" by dropping out of the thinking mind and into the Real Self. And the best is yet to come, as your gains come in. You begin to feel lighter and freer, and then upgrades happen in all areas of your life, almost like a by-product. Without even thinking about it, you may find that your love life falls into place. You move into a job you enjoy or start that business that you've been dreaming about. When I led my groups in London where we practised some of these tools together, I saw people looking so much better over time – and sometimes years younger, despite time passing. Regulars at the group often commented on this, too.

Having finished the four weeks, you may have some additional questions, which I'll endeavour to answer below. Still, I also recommend throwing any that I don't answer here to your *Higher Power List* to ask the source of all of the answers, your Higher Power, God, the Universe or whatever you want to call it – instead. It's amazing how, when you get on with your work (which is the "left-hand side" of the list – clearing your mind and appreciating life as best you can), the answers come to you. Sometimes directly through an insight, other times the answer pops up on the internet or a friend or colleague says something which answers your question. If you still think this sounds far-fetched – give it a go, and see how many of the dilemmas you throw on the right-hand side of the *Higher Power List* get sorted out, without you needing to think about it.

Start Small

Don't overload yourself with doing everything at once. I've heard people say from the get-go they are going to meditate for an hour every day, write 150 things they appreciate every day and also have a go at all the other techniques. They go from no routine at all to setting themselves several hours of tasks every day. When they inevitably don't do what they said they were going to do, they feel awful and want to give up, wondering why they've got no willpower.

Instead, introduce the new practices slowly. This way if you do miss doing what you said you were going to do, you can focus on one of these "small" things you actually have done, the feeling of this will encourage you to keep going. Self-criticism or getting mad at yourself for procrastinating doesn't stop you procrastinating. We all do it sometimes, and it's part of the process. Sometimes those who procrastinate the most at the beginning become the most disciplined of all. This makes sense when you realize (via the *Freedom Process*) that procrastination is the weightlift for discipline. So, you can embrace everything you do – or in this case, are not doing.

Daily Practice

Once you have figured out which of the techniques you prefer, make yourself a routine. First thing in the morning is a good time for *Focal-point Meditation* and a couple of the written techniques. As you do this, your new state of mind will become more automatic or natural and carry over for the whole day. You will naturally start looking for the good in your challenges and thus let them go.

It's all about practice. Those who do the work consistently get the best results – it is as simple as that, there's no magic formula. I saw this time and again at my weekly groups. The new tools become a new habit, and those other habits that haven't been working, fall away. When it comes to your routine, you want to experiment with the tools you've learned and see what appeals to you. We are all different, and different ones will click with you. However, here are some suggestions:

Start with *Focal-point Meditation*. The mind wants to rush into the more "fun" techniques, but this can be a trick. Without first clearing your mind, attempting some of the written practices, the mind chatter will get involved, and you won't be able to do it. And so first, meditate to build a foundation of clear-mindedness. (Remember you can check how long to meditate for using the *Higher Power List,* but if you're not sure, begin with 25 minutes, but don't be surprised if that number increases slightly as you are inspired to do more.)

It's best to start with a fixed amount of meditation and use a timer for it in the beginning, as the resistance from the mind chatter repeatedly telling you "you've done enough and it's time to stop" may be too great. After a while, you can be more flexible with your meditation.

You then might want to draft a *Higher Power List* and handover any problematic thoughts about the day ahead to the right-hand side. Any relationships on your mind, issues or meetings you have. For example: "Sort out my relationship with ________", "Get me to the meeting on time", "Make the meeting go well", "Help me be more me no matter what", "Show me the next step to take", "Centre me in my Real Self", etc. If anyone is on your mind that you care about, you can add them on to your list too along with a specific request if necessary. Just drop all these thoughts on to the page – offload them.

In the beginning stages, the *Higher Power List* is certainly useful for adding your daily techniques on the left-hand "Me" side to remind you of what to do – and then to tick them off when you've done them. Some people like to replace the *Higher Power List* with the *Retrospective Process*, or at least interchange them depending on their mood. Others choose to make a *Higher Power List* only when they get overwhelmed, or a lot is going on that day – although some people swear by it as a daily practice.

Then go to a new page and make a gratitude list (see page 72). If there is some issue stopping you from freely doing this list, smooth things over with the *Freedom Process* or *"What's Good About…" List.* Remember, you are well on your way. For example, if you haven't got the job yet, love your life now and see the benefits of not having the job *this week*. After a while, the *"What's Good About…" List* will naturally flow into *Gratitude 150* – as you move from looking for the good in what you don't want to appreciating what you have and already like. In many ways, these lists are the same – they are just about focusing on different subjects.

Sometimes you will want to go straight into the *Confidence*

Evoke, which is a more specific way to do gratitude and focus on what's working. You may want to finish off with the *Retrospective Process,* handing over all those future dreams and desires you may have and then writing down what you are going to do now they have happened – now that you have achieved them.

Some days you may just want to stop with a *"What's Good About…" List* if you're not feeling so great. As a general rule, the later on in the course I teach the practices, the more designed they are for when you are feeling better. Refer to the reference chart on page 119 and you'll see the further down the list they appear, the best suited they are to a better mood.

And now, begin your day. If your mind is tempted to go into overthinking in those idle moments, like when you're walking somewhere or waiting in line or whatever, do *FreeSelf Anchors (Declarations)* to centre yourself and then go about your day. You can also use the *Icon Switch* to help overthinking instead, or the *Thought Neutralizer*. You will find which works best for you.

If You're Short of Time

On those days you're busy, do a short version of your usual routine. This isn't to replace your full practice – but it will tide you over until you are ready to resume. Create a shortened version to do on days like this – for example, meditation can be 20 minutes, along with a 20-item gratitude list. Create a shortened version for occasional use on days like this.

There really is no recipe as we are all different – so it's about finding out what works for you and then developing a regular practice, varying it every now and then as guided.

When to Use *FreeSelf Anchors (Declarations)* or *Icon Switch* for Intrusive Thoughts

These approaches are different, and almost opposite, so you really have to choose just one at a time when dealing with intrusive thoughts. Many people find it better to use *FreeSelf*

Anchors (Declarations) when they are already clear-minded and centred as a way of staying in that state throughout the day. I've seen people repeat declarations, trying to feel good and ending up feeling worse and defeated. If you can't stop thinking about a specific something or someone and you make declarations to "try to distract" yourself, then this resistance may make things worse as you try to "drown out" the thoughts with your declarations.

In this case – of specific thoughts that keep coming back – I'd say, "what if these thoughts are a necessary workout, so not to be armoured against, but utilized – maybe they are there for a reason." And so I suggest you use the *Icon Switch,* letting the thoughts happen and overlaying the thoughts with your icon, reminding you of the gains. However, as I repeatedly say – don't make this a rule. Some people use *FreeSelf Anchors (Declarations)* whatever their mood and it helps give them something to focus on when their snow globe is shaken up with thoughts so much that they can't meditate. The phrase gives them something more tangible than a sound to hold on to. While they repeat the phrase over and over, they bring to mind a huge ship's anchor or a ship's mast and see the phrase as something real to hold on to and stay centred – and they find it easier to meditate this way if their mind is particularly busy. And other people use the *Thought Neutralizer,* which is a similar approach to *FreeSelf Anchors (Declarations),* using the specific declaration of "Thank you". It really is something you will want to experiment with and find which technique works best for you in each situation. Try all the practices out, and you will come up with a specific routine that works for you.

FreeSelf Anchors (Declarations) are not a weapon to battle thoughts: they are an armour to protect you from thoughts. The *Icon Switch* is for repetitive, specific intrusive thoughts that you have been dealing with for some time.

Feeling Worse Before You Feel Better?

Sometimes when you use these techniques and processes, it can initially seem things are not getting better – but they are. You may find that you hit a "cloudbank" of intense storms of overthinking, but don't be put off. This is a positive sign – it's a cleansing or detox of all the old overthinking patterns. Rather than battle, go with it. Remind yourself the unwanted patterns are being cleansed and released and it's a good thing. And don't be afraid of thoughts or see them as wrong. Although they are not the source of your guidance, they are valid resistance training which help you evolve. Your job isn't to get rid of them but learn how to work with them rather than be ruled by them – as this book will show you.

Take your time with each technique, not rushing, but continuing to move through them. In other words, get OK with where you are, but as soon as you have, move on to a technique taught later in the course.

It's not about getting rid of the resistance but working with the resistance.

When you're about to begin something new and even on a roll, feeling amazing, don't be surprised if you find yourself waking up in the opposite mood. You may have a run of feeling you are living a dream life, and then you wake up feeling awful and like you'll never get anywhere. This is natural, like an Olympic champion increasing their weights at the gym. The weights are coming to take you higher. Most people try to fight the weights; they feel deflated and "try" to feel confident (which is just resistance against the low feeling, and what you resist, persists). When you get excited with the processes in this book, you are going to hit the weights. Be prepared for it. It's a *good* thing.

I remember one coaching client who was excited about the prospect of the start of the year because he wanted it to be his best ever. He had a great business idea and was excited about making it happen. And he was really getting into some of the techniques. However, at the start of January, I got a message from him wanting to book a session. He was feeling awful – like a failure and like it was never going to happen. I reminded him this was OK. What if he needed this drop to jump higher? What if the feeling of failure was necessary to weightlift its opposite – success? In making friends with this feeling, he felt enthusiastic again in a very short time – a matter of hours. In fact, he felt better than he had before. He realized that this low was the feeling of the workout for his best year yet. And it turned out that it *was* his best year yet.

The key with the tools is to help you feel better no matter what: to get you to that place where you feel you have all you need right now. It's to get rid of those desires which are in the way of you loving your life today. This won't get rid of your dreams – it will get rid of the obstacles that are in the way of your dreams.

It's OK to feel down. It's OK to feel defeated. This drop is like dropping into a set of push-ups to take you to the next level. A drop in emotion is just a weightlift to take you to the next level.

Which Technique for When?

In general, the tools at the top of the following reference chart can be done in all moods – though you'll probably only want to do them when you are feeling low. The tools toward the bottom of the chart are for when you are feeling good. But, we are all different, so try them out for yourself and see what works for you.

REFERENCE CHART	
Emotional Overwhelm Tools and Practices (see page 47)	Simple exercises for when you're experiencing overthinking and challenging emotions.
Rapids Float (see page 50)	Hold the cushion and relax into your mood.
Icon Switch (see page 52)	Overlay the workout with an image of the gains.
Thought Neutralizer (see page 56)	Keep your atmosphere free of mind chatter by "spraying" the space around you.
Relationship Trigger (see page 91)	Bring your attention from the difficult relationship to give unconditional attention to the person within you.
Focal-point Meditation (see page 40)	Focus on an object while you tune into your Real Self.
Higher Power List (see page 36)	Surrender all your problems and issues to a Higher Power.
Magic Button (see page 88)	Press the button and call your power back through realizing it's the feeling you want first, more than the change in the situation.
Freedom Process (see page 68)	Identify the gains from your workout and then embrace the workout to get instant freedom from your blocks.
"What's Good About…" List (see page 61)	Focus on the good in the problem to release it.
FreeSelf Anchors (Declarations) (see page 96)	Keep your mind clear by filling up the space with words spoken aloud or in your mind.
Self-realization Process (see page 82)	Acknowledging the person that you are through looking into your eyes in a mirror/reflective surface.
Gratitude 150 (see page 72)	Appreciate your life and dwell on all the details that are working for you with this extended list.

REFERENCE CHART	
Confidence Evoke (see page 77)	Recalling those moments that you were successful in a specific area of your life and then spending time feeling them in the present moment.
Retrospective Process (page 100)	Write down what you are going to do assuming that you've achieved your goals and are living your ideal life already.
Starboard (see page 104)	Create an artboard or chart to remind you of all those interests which get your attention, engage and excite you.

PART III
RELATIONSHIPS AND SELF-CONFIDENCE

CHAPTER 1

LOOKING AND FEELING YOUR BEST SELF

Feel attractive, no matter what.

People can get very self-critical about their bodies, disliking the way they look and constantly trying to fix or improve their appearance. If something isn't working out and you've gone into overthinking, body image is one of the first places your mind is likely to go – attacking your appearance, blaming the rejection, for example, on not being attractive enough, young-looking enough, and so on.

You may think that taking time to focus on looking good is shallow – but it's really not. Especially nowadays, so many of us get into overthinking on the subject of physical appearance because it's everywhere on social media and the media in general. Body image issues can make us miserable and affect all areas of life, so it's a vital thing to get it sorted out so you can forget about it and move on.

Outer Beauty Is About an Inner Shift

The conventional approach to fix or change *outer* looks above all else doesn't work very well. The simple truth here is that if you don't know how to feel better from within, then you may end up fixing one thing and then moving on to fixing more and more. Makeovers are great and certainly can give a confidence boost, but without that strong sustained inner confidence, the outer makeover won't ever be enough. Beauty really does come from within. It is an attitude: a manifestation of inner confidence.

When it comes to attraction, we tend to think we are admiring physical appearance, but it actually has a lot more to do with that person's self-perception mirrored outward. In other words, if someone knows they are attractive, they are. And so being attractive is simply *feeling* attractive. The common factor shared by people who are considered to be beautiful is that they *feel* beautiful, or believe they are beautiful on some level; *confidence is their common denominator.*

Being beautiful is feeling beautiful. And that's it.

Beauty is about how attractive you *feel* you are, rather than anything else. It's not about thinking beautiful thoughts or thinking about beauty. It's not about *thinking;* it's about the space between thoughts. When you *feel* beautiful, you are not in the mode of thinking, you are *being*. In other words – it's all another way of saying "confidence". And this state of confidence is the answer that you're looking for, on all subjects, actually. We all know this on some level; we can see how confidence wins every time.

Those who are considered beautiful can be totally physically different – especially across eras and cultures – so there is no point in obsessing about your own individual features. Your own particular features do not necessarily make you beautiful or not beautiful, and they become a distraction from what it's really about for many people. So, you want to zoom out and find a way to feel beautiful in general. All the details will sort themselves out when you *feel* beautiful.

You may believe that feeling beautiful is simply delusional, but this is not the case. Feeling attractive creates its own atmosphere and its own reality. It may not mean everyone on the planet agrees (as it's also about what *they* are seeing – hence the phrase "beauty is in the eye of the beholder"). But when you *feel* beautiful, you don't care so much what others think of your looks anyway – as you only cared about that when you *didn't* feel attractive.

Are Looks Fixed?

Many people believe looks are fixed, and we might be able to smile more or improve our posture but, apart from surgery, that's about it. This isn't true at all. Increasing self-confidence around body image can actually improve our physical appearance. It sounds unbelievable – but I have seen this again and again. Better still, the great *feeling* of being beautiful is the reason you wanted to *be* beautiful in the first place, and as you will learn, you can get this feeling before any changes actually occur.

Being attractive and feeling attractive are the same thing.

After reading this, you may be rushing to "try" to feel attractive and wondering how to do that. Remind yourself that it does take work to drop into that constant feeling of inner confidence, so trying to dive into feeling like a supermodel will probably backfire and make you feel even worse. Inner confidence is always there for you at your centre – which is especially soothing to know in a world that can tell you you're not enough – and there's a method to realize that state of confidence which I'll explain.

I've met people whose days can be absolutely ruined by seeing a bad reflection in the mirror. Or sometimes it's seeing a bad photo of themselves that can be that thing that gets them off-centre. They check their image, take "selfie" camera shots of themselves over and over, from all different angles. They obsess. They think about it all day long. Some people even see the same photo of themselves and in one moment think they look great in it – and then in the next, not so good, or worse. This makes no logical sense – but again shows that it's all about perception, not anything fixed.

Have you ever looked in the mirror on different occasions and seen completely different images? Everyone knows this. Sometimes you see yourself as attractive, and at other times you see yourself as not attractive at all. This is the point I am trying to make here. Looking in the mirror is no measure of how beautiful you are because the mirror image reflects back how you are *feeling*, far more than it shows you anything else.

So, step away from mirrors as a means to focus on your outer body for a while. When you do have to look, when getting ready, for example, keep it brief and look "in outline", meaning don't zoom in. Analysing your body is nothing more than overthinking, which, as you've learned in this book, just clouds over your Real Self. This is an important first step: Avoiding mirrors, for the time being, will allow you to let loose of the nightmare mood. So first, do your workout, do your meditation, follow the four-week course – do what it takes to get you "in" to your Real Self *and then look.*

The exception is when you're doing the *Self-realization Process* (see page 82) because that technique is not about studying and critiquing the outer body: it's about using your eyes to make a loving connection with the person within you. Though, if you are too involved with obsessive thoughts about your appearance, this process might not be the best one to go to right away, as the temptation to look at your physical body and criticize it may be too strong.

Accepting Where You Are – *What's Good About* Not Liking Your Appearance?

So you want to be attractive, but you don't feel attractive. The first place is to start with where you are. You might feel so far off feeling beautiful that you just think it's never going to happen. Remember, it's perfectly OK to feel unattractive. And it had better be OK because sometimes everyone *does* feel unattractive. Don't try to pretend you feel beautiful or handsome when you clearly don't feel it. You feel how you feel about the subject, and that's OK.

What is OK about this? *What's Good About it?* Well, this practice gets us to *evolve* to more beauty (see also page 61). It is the workout for beauty, in fact. The most beautiful people have felt the most unattractive at times in their life – or at least felt a lot of insecurity on this subject. It's all OK.

It's OK to have bad days and feel unattractive – it's evolving your beauty.

And so when you find yourself feeling unattractive, remind yourself that it's OK; it's normal – everyone feels this at times. It is causing you to evolve. It's showing you how important this subject is for you. If you didn't feel any tension at all, it wouldn't be a possibility for you to be beautiful because remember that the "low points" evolve you to the best of life in specific areas.

You may even decide that you *absolutely, definitely* look unattractive – and it's a fact. The thing is you are right on this level of thought. When you are in the "lower-self mind" it seems factual. But when the thoughts clear, you experience something different. For example: *What's Good About* not liking your appearance could be:

- *I'm not the only one who has felt this way about body image – and it's OK to feel this.*
- *It's getting me to join the gym (something that you may have been putting off, but you've really wanted to do, and this nudge of not feeling good is simply to do it).*
- *It has made me take care of myself and discover a new approach. It shows that I do care about my appearance.*
- *It has made me look for solutions, and perhaps it will help me to find solutions. It has given me compassion and understanding for others in this position.*
- *Every time I feel unattractive, I am evolving, and creating the possibility to be more attractive.*
- *Many people who at different times in their life felt very unattractive are now extremely attractive people.*
- *I have witnessed famous people like (mention name) completely changing their appearance through new habits, so I know it is possible.*
- *It has created the thrust to be more beautiful.*

For example, *What's Good About* seeing a bad photo could be:

- *It is getting me to be OK with things.*
- *Every time I see an unattractive picture, it is evolving me to be better looking.*
- *Seeing that photo is a nudge for me to really give these processes/ techniques a go.*
- *Other people like the photo so perhaps it is showing me it's just my perception – and now I'm being nudged to work on shifting my perspective.*
- *It is kind of funny how I can see myself in all different ways, and it does seem to mirror my mood and nudge me to do the four-week course in this book to feel more connected and confident!*

Now you've accepted where you are – realizing that where you are is the perfect workout to the beautiful you – we are going to move on with one of the best techniques I know to develop a strong and positive body image.

Confidence Evoke Revisited – Dwelling on Compliments

Your opinion of you is what people respond to. Compliments are ultimately people telling you your own beliefs about yourself. For example, that new outfit you looked great in that everyone said you looked great in – you might have played it down, but you *knew* you looked good, right? We always do, on some level. Similarly, when we are being down on ourselves and think we "need" compliments, they are hard to come by, as life is again mirroring back our opinion of ourselves – in this case, an uncomplimentary opinion in the form of no compliments at all.

And so *you* have to go first in feeling attractive rather than waiting for the world, other people or even mirrors to show you that you are attractive. This technique is all about you giving yourself the confidence you have been looking for from the world. It will show you that you are probably a lot closer to what you want than you think – but the clouds of self-doubt are in the way. We get a compliment, and ten seconds later we forget it and go into self-criticism – we feel happy for a second and then move on into mind chatter, forgetting about the compliment almost instantly. This is a waste. Instead, go over those compliments again and again – really revel in them.

> Compliments from others that we really felt good about and compliments about ourselves are gold – and we want to recall them and revel in them, over and over.

The *Confidence Evoke* (see page 77) is about evoking those moments or memories when you felt great. Here's how to do it.

Write down your Affirmative Statement, which is a sentence or a paragraph describing how you would look, if you could wave a magic wand: "*I am incredibly attractive*" might be a start.

Underneath write down all the times you've felt what you've written in the statement. In this case, "I am incredibly attractive", is about remembering all the times you felt attractive, or were complimented on your appearance and felt good because of those compliments. You may not have felt exactly like the statement – but do your best to feel close. List all the times you looked good and knew that you did – go over and over those compliments that you've had.

Evoke the memories of those times you felt attractive as you write them down. For example, "When I walked down the beachfront, I felt like a goddess", "Jasmine said I looked like a model," etc. Of course, your lower-self mind may counter with, "Oh, I was younger then." However, it is not the age, but the feeling of being beautiful that makes someone attractive. Remember, there are people who, like we all ought to, feel better about themselves and actually look better and even younger the more time passes. But see how you feel – only choose to evoke those situations that actually make you feel beautiful.

You will look better when you feel that you look better. It's as simple as that. If you feel you are attractive, you are. People just mirror back how you feel about yourself. For example:

Affirmative Statement: "I am incredibly attractive, confident, model-like, magnetic and make an impact wherever I go."

- *When I walked down the street, and I sensed those people admiring me.*
- *Sasha said my new outfit looked really good.*
- *When I wore the suit, Lee said I looked like a model.*
- *When I saw myself in the mirror in the changing room, I looked really attractive.*
- *I was in the café, and that woman came up to me and said I looked like a movie star.*

When making your list, remember that it's less about what words you use and more about taking time to conjure the feeling you had at that time.

It doesn't so much matter what wording you use in the sentences you are writing. The key is that as you write, you evoke a memory. You want to spend a few moments on each sentence before you move on to anchoring in that feeling of being attractive – or the feeling of whatever it is you've written for your Affirmative Statement.

Some people may only be able to find one or two things. But don't give up. What I've found is this is doable for everyone – just one or two things you can feel will "grow" into more. As you make this list regularly, it will get easier the more times you do it: you will recall more times you felt beautiful and notice more times in your day when you feel beautiful.

Do *Confidence Evoke* When You're Already Feeling OK

Another important note is to do this technique when you are already feeling OK, don't do it when you are feeling low about the subject of body image. In that case, try one of the practices such as one of the *Emotional Overwhelm Tools and Practices* from Week 1 (see page 47) or *Focal-point Meditation* (see page 40) or do your *"What's Good About..." List* (see page 61) about not feeling attractive, to get yourself in "neutral" – clear-minded and ready to begin.

I know an actor who wrote "star quality" as his Affirmative Statement. When I saw him at the group again, he had real movie star presence – he exuded confidence. A few months later I saw him in a charismatic lead role in a popular TV series, and he was certainly a star.

I remember another one of my group participants doing this process. She had turned up for the first time, totally depressed. She heard something in what I was saying, and I didn't see her for about six months. When she returned, she was unrecognizable. She looked totally different, years younger, attractive, her stance was different and yet I knew it was her. She said it was all down to this particular technique. Someone asked her disbelievingly "Well, I'm sure you dieted" and she said "Yes, I did change my diet – but I've been dieting for 20 years and got virtually no results. It was this technique that opened the route to a diet that actually worked. I felt attractive for the first time." She acknowledged that it was very difficult, to begin with. But after a week or so it got easier.

People in the group wondered why the technique didn't work as well for them, but I quickly realized it was simply that she did the technique every day – and they didn't. Consistency is key.

Another man couldn't get a date, and he felt it was because he was "too ugly". And so, he did this practice. He went along to his local café and started remembering and listing all the times he had received compliments and really felt attractive. After a few weeks, he was, in his words, "more popular than he'd ever been" as far as admiring looks etc. He told me that he had been in the café doing this particular process when a man who he had been exchanging glances with approached him and left a nice note with his phone number. "This never happens to me," he said – but a few weeks later, he got asked out again. This process may seem almost like magic, but it's very simple – life tends to respond to how you feel about yourself. He felt attractive, and the world agreed with his self-opinion.

Comparison

When you see someone attractive, your lower-self can try to diminish you. That's the normal response for most people – to feel less than. First, be OK with feeling envy (*"What's Good About…"* is showing me what I want and what, in truth, I am, etc.) to free yourself and then you can move on. You will find that when you get a handle on what I'm sharing in this book, attractive people will inspire you and you won't shrink, but you'll stand taller, feeling happy that you've seen beauty and enriched because of it. Your envy will turn to being energized and having the feeling of "that's for me": that you can take the attractiveness they are "owning" and be that too.

Other Things You Can Do to Feel Attractive, No Matter What

Remember to add regular *Focal-point Meditation* (see page 40). Your perception is everything, and meditation shifts your world in this way. Someone I was coaching told me: "I turned up to a modelling job, and I looked in the mirror, and I looked terrible – and also like I'd put on 10lbs! This wasn't possible, I thought – but there I was. Then I remembered to meditate. As much as I didn't want to, I knew this would work. I meditated for half an hour, and when I noticed myself in the mirror again, I looked completely different, like the me that had got the job to begin with."

Get good at the *Self-realization Process* (see page 82). When you love the person within you, your inner beauty glows and affects the outer body. You feel beautiful – and so you are.

The Power of Posture

Once you've found a bit of peace about how you're feeling, certain actions may get you to feel more attractive. You can buy new clothes, get a haircut. What is more important than what these actions physically do is how they make you feel. Being active will shunt you out of being stuck in the repetitive, "broken record" thoughts of not liking yourself. But there is something else you can do that will really shift things. It sounds so obvious, but one of the best instant shifts you can do is with your posture. People with a poor body image and lack of confidence don't stand tall – by standing tall and walking tall this physically brings out the best in you, and it gives you a vibe of confidence. It clears your mind and gets you in touch with confident feelings (it's harder to be down on yourself when standing and walking tall, shoulders back and chest out – try it and see).

More Exercises for a Better Body Image

When people ask me for any additional, body image-focused recommendations to explore alongside this book, I suggest face exercises. They are similar to gentle gym exercises for the facial muscles, meaning you deliberately contract and relax the muscles in specific exercises. It makes sense to me how they could smooth and tone the face. I've also heard proponents of similar exercises for the scalp explain how they can be beneficial for good hair growth.

I can see how these approaches, at the very least, are a good way to relax. The repetitive movements are relaxing, and become like *Focal-point Meditation* (see page 40), in a similar way that doing exercises at the gym does. Plus, I have heard many favourable testimonials. If you search online, you will find people who specialize in these areas along with their methods.

CHAPTER 2

WELLNESS, HEALTH AND HEALING

We are way more powerful than we know.

No one knows exactly how the body works. It's a great mystery – and it's infinitely more incredible than the best piece of equipment we could make. Our current theories may be impressive and at times useful, but only in proportion to what we currently know. And what we think we know is tiny in the scheme of things and will change as all scientific understanding does.

You are incredibly powerful, and it's time to start seeing yourself that way, rather than as a weak, faulty machine in need of constant interference (meaning our overthinking "fix it" mindset). What if the intelligence behind the body always knew what to do and always did the right thing, intending to bring you the best life experience for the moment through new insights gained from every experience? What if when you think something's going wrong, it's actually a misunderstanding of a complex process of healing, where your body is evolving to a stronger, more resilient and powerful place – and it's something to be grateful for, not fearful about?

No one ought to be blamed for a health issue but appreciated for finding an avenue to sort out their lives, as this is one way of looking at really what's going on, rather than that "something's gone wrong".

In short, experiencing good health is about finding a way to trust and believe in the great power of who you are.

Relaxing into the Self Gives Space for Healing to Arise

When you relax, you allow the intelligence behind the body to do its incredible job. And you also give any people who are supporting your health space to do their job too. When you are relaxed, meaning you are clear-minded and centred, healing happens because the door to wellness opens. Healing is less of a trying to get rid of something or trying to make better or battle against anything, and more of a door opening to the health that is already there.

However, even this suggestion can cause stress, and can make you feel like you need to try to relax when you are totally stressed out. Stress isn't so much the problem – it's battling against stress. But even battling against stress is alright, and it is understandable to want to battle it. It's all OK. And so, if you are stressed, it's alright, and you are still very much on the path. You want to love yourself anyway and make friends with those stressful feelings first, which will naturally open the way for relaxation. Often the healing process involves lots of stress initially – and that's OK. It's better than just OK though – it's the workout for the healing.

Perhaps you feel worried about your health. Pain and other health symptoms can cause your lower-self mind to race into illusion, and your Real Self is covered in the clouds of overthinking. Remember, this is a workout, but you are not your lower-self mind, and it is time to release yourself from thoughts and drop into the knowing of your Real Self. In this place, healing is waiting to be discovered – all kinds of solutions are waiting, in fact, right in this moment. You just want to let the snow globe settle; let the thoughts settle *and listen.*

Let the thoughts settle and listen for guidance.

When you experience a health issue or unexpected symptom, the mind chatter can go "off on one" and lead you to Google. This is never a good idea when you're not feeling yourself as you've probably already realized – as you tend to just find more and more things to get worried about and get trapped in a cyclone of mind chatter which blocks the solutions you seek. You just can't find anything useful when you are in fearful overthinking. But before you can distract, you have to settle into where you are right now and not fight against your mood. "Trying to not think" about what you're thinking about can lead to obsessing about it even more.

Is it Denial or Awareness?

There's a huge difference between "changing your channel" from fear to empowerment and denial. Denial is pretending you feel different than you do. So denial would be feeling frightened about a situation while pretending everything was OK, trying to ignore it and trying to put "perfect health" thoughts on top of the whirlwind of fear – and then not going to a doctor or health practitioner but secretly thinking you should go. This constant feeling of dread is a sure sign that you are out of your Real Self – and it's not what I'm talking about. It's a huge exercise in resistance and, in that state, you are never clear enough to make the right decision. *So first, settle.* Clear your mind so you can see the path to take; the path that is already there, obscured by your overthinking. You will know when you have achieved this when you begin to feel lighter and more clear-minded. Then you can start seeing where you are and will know what actions to take.

Choosing the Best Path for You

If you need support, I'm not one of these people to say choose one method or another – there are testimonials of incredible healing which people attribute with all kinds of approaches. That said, the one thing I will say about healing is this – regardless of which practitioner you go to or which physical system you choose – a theme in the healing stories I've heard is when people get into that clear-minded Real Self state. It is just the same on the subject of health as it is with all subjects.

We are all different – and this book is about realising that within, you know what to do – your Real Self knows, and your intuition knows. It's about using the only real power of choice you do have – to drop into your centre no matter what is going on. From this clear space, you will know what to do. The right information is all around you; you will hear the right information at the right time when you are in your Real Self. What I've found is when people do practices similar to the ones I share in this book and find peace of mind, they know what to do. They make good choices.

It's about finding that Real Self state and discovering the wellness that is there for you.

And it's not "either/or". You can make an appointment to see your health practitioner while also doing the techniques in this book or similar. You can do your part, doing the techniques in this book to soothe your own emotions and sort out your (over) thinking and your stress – and then you can let those health practitioners with specific expertise do their part.

What I will say though is this – people who are in their Real Self are always more uplifting, aren't they? Confident, optimistic, can-do people who are championing you; those reassuring practitioners who can tell you – and mean it – that it's OK and things are going to work out fine. Scaring people with an opinion never accomplishes anything. And everything is an opinion. If for some reason, you end up with a real pessimist in the medical field, meet them with the practices in this book. You want to see that person for the gift that they, too, are. If you are annoyed at someone for being negative, you could use the *"What's Good About..." List* to be OK with your reaction – and even with them. A good thing about being scared by an opinion is that "I should have been told that because I was" and "Perhaps I needed to hear it to get me to *really* find my own strength and power within and stop giving my power away to random people outside of me."

It's going to be OK.

Relaxing into the Perfect Health That's Here Now

The body will certainly appreciate your getting into your Real Self. And it is in this state of inner stillness and just "being" that so-called miracles happen.

From researching many stories of "miracle healings" – and also speaking to various medical doctors and alternative practitioners about this subject – the common denominator seems to be that healings tend to happen when we finally find a way to be a bit more relaxed and accepting about where we are. This isn't resignation or a "giving up" (which is simply overthinking) – it's a surrender into that space of clear-minded peace. It is relaxing into knowing that it's OK – and it's going to be OK. It's a shift in perception. The person in this situation is less manically trying to heal and more loving themselves no matter what – which admittedly can be easier said than done in these situations. Just like finding a relationship and all the other good stuff, healing tends to happen when you're not trying so hard to get a result.

Right now, you are loved, and you can relax into this Divine Love.

And of course, before every amazing healing story, there is often a lot of worries and battling and trying to heal which went on for some time. And that's OK. It's often a necessary part of the healing, in fact. And so, the healing journey is often like this: First there's the workout of worry. Then, there is relaxation – and then the door opens to healing.

Stress Is Not Stressful

Being told stress is bad for you is… stressful. It might make you feel like you shouldn't be stressed or worry what the stress is doing to you – which piles on the worry and creates more stress. As you now know, stress is a workout with benefits. The irony is, when we make friends with stress, we stop being so stressed. So even if you believe that stress is absolutely not good for you at all – still, the way to drop it is to embrace and accept it. The first step to getting rid of stress is to embrace it, just as it is.

And so first, be OK with your emotional reaction about what's happening: your emotional reaction to any health condition or label or fearful thoughts. Then – and often only then – can you be OK about what's happening, which includes looking for the good in the condition itself.

What's Good About Stress

Stress and the situation itself may be nudging you to shift your life in a way you will love – it might be giving you just the nudge you need. Or perhaps the situation is creating gains and strengthening you in ways you can't see right now. There are many ways to look at the same situation. What if things are going right? This is your task: to find out why that statement is true.

I explain that stress is a workout, and it's a sign you're on track to the solution. However, after a while, you know that stress isn't helping, but you're not letting it go – why? It may be because it can be difficult to jump into "*What's Good About...*" (see page 61) having this condition when it comes to having an illness. So, you want to start with where you are, which may be: "You are allowed not to worry, you are allowed to let it go."

1. "*What's Good About* Being Afraid"

- *Many people would overthink and be afraid or worry in this situation – especially with all the negative news stories about health. I'm doing OK.*
- *It's OK to be stressed – it's evolving more relaxation and happiness.*
- *I should be feeling afraid right now – because that's how I feel.*
- *What if the worry was a necessary ingredient to evolve me to better health?*

All of this is not the easiest when you are in the middle of physical symptoms and fear. You may instead choose to do a *Freedom Process* (see page 68) on this subject – and the *Emotional Overwhelm Tools and Practices* (see page 47) would work too, as a general way to soothe you. Or the *Higher Power List* (see page 36). You will find the right one for you. You might be drawn to different practices at different times. You could even open this book at random in the course section, begin reading, and see if it speaks to you.

What if nothing is going wrong, but everything is going right, and I just can't see it yet?

2. "*What's Good About* Having This Condition"

Right at this moment, you may not be able to change whatever health condition that you are going through, but you *can* change your perspective. There is a different way of looking at health conditions where, rather than seeing things as going wrong, you realize that everything can be used as a tool in our evolution. Perhaps health conditions are actually a method of healing our lives: a signal to us to adjust our perspective? In other words, perhaps this body has such ingenious intelligence behind it that if it truly wanted to come into balance, it would do so? And if it hasn't, nothing has gone wrong either. Perhaps this situation or condition is bringing you a message – the message to help you love yourself more and live life to the fullest. But reading my suggestions, which soothe me, may not work for you. When it comes to the *"What's Good About..." List,* the power is you finding what soothes *you*. You want to find your own insights. So, take some time on this list – perhaps do it after you've meditated – and see what comes to you. Set yourself a challenge that you are going to look for the good in this condition just as it is – no matter what – and wait for new perspectives to come to you, and then write them down. For example:

- *It has made me take better care of myself and discover a new approach to living well.*
- *This condition has made me look for solutions. Perhaps it's here to help me find solutions – and even help others in my situation.*
- *All negatives are weightlifts – it's a weightlift to better health.*
- *It is strengthening my body and mind.*
- *It's forced me to go within and find my Real Self power – and really know that that's the most powerful force.*

Or if this condition is an injury:

- *This should have happened because it did.*
- *Perhaps it happened to give me a rest from the gym, which may be good for my body in general.*
- *It has forced me to commit to meditating every day.*
- *It has altered my morning routine by putting the gym on pause, which got me to go to a different area of town to meet this friend I wouldn't have met otherwise – perhaps it happened for that.*

Healthy Eating and Mental Diets

Healthy eating advice can be confusing; there seems to be a new best-ever diet out each week, which sometimes totally contradicts the last one. And then you see that there are "healthy eaters" following strict diets who are not healthy at all – and people who eat junk food and seem to be in glowing health. What is possibly more important than the food we eat is the way we feel about the food we eat. In other words, eat the foods you believe are best for you to eat – we all have our inner knowing.

Following a certain diet can be beneficial, but if you are in your overthinking, inner battle state, it's like putting the best raw material into a broken refinery. People forget to prioritize their *mental diet*, which is the "diet" where you exclude thoughts. Get into your Real Self first using this book, and then you will be guided to look after the rest of everything perfectly for you –

which will include the right fitness, the right food to eat and the right actions for you to take.

A Guided Journey for Wellness: Healing Sanctuary

I sometimes record guided journeys like this one for people I'm coaching, so that they can put the audio on and take a lie down to clear their mind when any challenges come up on the subject of, in this case, wellness. You can record it for yourself, with some music in the background. Or you can listen to it on the audiobook version.

1. Get yourself comfortable, sitting or lying down in a chair or on a bed, without any other distractions around.
2. In your mind's eye, feel yourself relaxing on a soft, comfortable bed in the middle of a small boat – and you are surrounded by guides, angels, or whatever beings bring comfort to you.
3. Relax as the boat begins to move through the still, calm lake. You are moving toward this fern-covered healing clearing. You move into this clearing, secluded and private, surrounded by trees, and the boat stops at a mooring.
4. Relaxing into the arms of your Real Self for a while, stepping back from your thinking mind, relaxing on this soft, comfortable bed on the boat.
5. The boat is surrounded by beings of light. Great healers and teachers surround you, the best of the best, experts in their field. Relax and let them do their work. Like a race car driver has to step aside to allow the mechanics to renew and refresh the car, take this time to relax into where you are.
6. One of the beings pours a divine elixir over you, which is like warm honey in its consistency and glowing, absorbing into your body and filling it with liquid light. Feel this liquid pouring, into your toes, your feet and moving up into your ankles, calves, your knees, your thighs, moving upward into your belly, your chest, your neck, all down your arms and into your fingertips. Feel this light moving up, feel this

light flushing out of your body all of the impurities, a darker stream is emitted into the waters around you to be purified and you feel refreshed and happy.

7. Now, one of the guides places a face pack made of the purest water gently on your face – it is cleansing and beautifying, feeling soothing and revitalizing.
8. And as you lie here now, relaxing and breathing slowly and deeply, a piece of equipment is brought out by the guides. Imagine a circular hovering device – like a ring which surrounds you – emitting light rays through your body as it moves slowly up your body, from your toes to the top of your head. Feel the power of this device which both aligns and attunes your body back to perfection.
9. Breathe into the sound in the background of this recording. Feel the equipment moving – up and down your body up and down your body. Breathe in… and breathe out. Feeling this device moving up and down your body renewing and refreshing and making it anew, every cell coming into sparkling balance.
10. Know you are safe with all these guides around you; you are safe to close your eyes, to relax deeper into the bed beneath you. And just let this device do its work, moving up and down your body from your feet to the top of your head, and back again. Feeling now, these rainbow-coloured light beams projecting through your body, feeling it bringing it into perfect alignment, perfection, renewing your mind, cells sparkling, everything perfection.
11. And bringing your attention back to your breathing – allow this equipment to do its work. This incredible piece of equipment that brings the body to perfection, your only job is to relax and breathe and focus on the sound being held by that sound in the background of this recording. Imagine this circular device moving up your body with its light rays going through your body. Feel the power of this equipment, which aligns and balances your body. Your whole body is attuned back to perfection.

12. This device moves up and down your body. Sparkling cells, perfection. Everything aligned and perfect. Every place the light touches is moved into perfect alignment, perfection. Your skin and all through your body to perfection. Youthening, balancing, beautifying, bringing you into alignment, as this device moves up and down your body.
13. When you feel that the device has done its work, the boat is unmoored and moves out of this cool, calm sanctuary out of the entrance through the ferns and out into the waters and back toward the riverbank where you started.
14. And as the boat gets to the bank just allow it to be moored again. And when you're ready, take a few deep breaths in and out. Slightly moving your body. Thanking the guides for the process, feeling amazing and opening your eyes.

Note: With the device I mention in this guided journey, some people like to imagine it working on them when they are in bed at night, or even when they are in a café as they sit and work – or are out and about. In their mind's eye, the circular ring doughnut-shaped device goes up and down their body as they work, sending white light or rainbow rays through their body from all sides – from the top of their head to their toes and back again – and they can "leave it on" for as long as they want. Some people choose different device "programs" such as an energizing "cartridge", which gives them more energy, or a beautifying "cartridge", making them more attractive – choosing a subject that makes them feel good. Or even a "three-in-one" which does it all.

CHAPTER 3

THE SEARCH FOR LOVE: DATING AND RELATIONSHIPS

Everything is about relationships. And every relationship is about your relationship with Self.

Relationships are a big part of our lives. And yet they can be the source of so much confusion and frustration and difficulty. People put a huge amount of time and effort into searching for someone to spend the rest of their life with. And then once they meet them, sometimes that's just the beginning of more problems. But it can be easier, as you'll discover here.

Dating

Everything you see around you in terms of advertisements, movies, music and general culture seems geared to get people focused on meeting "the one" – as if that's going to immediately solve everything. There are thousands of online dating agencies or apps with more added each week, in addition to the various self-help systems pledging to help you find love and meet your dating match. All of these new ways to find a partner haven't made things easier, they've simply increased our workload and overthinking; getting us to try harder to get something we think we desperately need and wonder if we are looking in the right place. It's like increasing a shop's floor space exponentially without increasing the number of items you actually want – the result is searching for love becomes a vast, almost full-time job.

You may be asking, "How do I stop looking for love?"

"You find love when you're not looking" can be an annoying phrase – but there's truth in it. Love happens when you're less desperately searching for love, when you're not overthinking it. So instead, you want to get a hobby more dynamic than your search for love. Use the *Higher Power List* for this – write down "bring me a dynamic hobby" on the right-hand side (see page 36) I've seen this work wonders for people.

All of this desperate searching for love can lead to less *self*-love – and without this self-acceptance, all the dating apps in the world will just mirror back this feeling in terms of experience. When you find peace of mind, you are clearer about the best avenues to go down. And it may be one of those online apps – or it might not be. But you will be clear minded rather than desperately searching; you will be surer of what's best for you. You will know what to do and get those inner nudges that guide you to those "right place right time" meetings.

When it comes to finding love, it is your state of being that matters more than anything else.

If you do feel needy, then find a way to make friends with your neediness. Let yourself be needy and desperate if that's what you are being – it simply may be the workout you require right now. Neediness is the weightlift for its opposite: self-sufficiency, strength and independence. It's also the workout for a great relationship. "*What's Good About* being needy" could be: "It's OK to long for love. It shows I care about meeting someone – it shows my ambition for love. So many people who are now with their soulmate probably felt intense longing and neediness. The fact that I feel this means I'm going to meet my 'one', for sure."

How to Get into the *Not* Looking for Love Vibe

And now you have cleared your feelings of neediness through accepting yourself exactly as you are (and accepting your feelings exactly as they are), you want to love the situation you're in. But you also want to *love being single.* It's as simple as that. If you don't love being single when you *are* single right now, you do not really love yourself.

When I facilitated a series of popular relationship-themed workshops called "Finding Love", I found that what I've just shared was one of the most effective approaches – to get a hobby more exciting than the search for love and also to fall in love with being single. More than a few attendees told me several months after the workshops they had met their significant other through these two practices.

Loving being single means you're not longing for love, which is your main block to finding love.

There is this idea that finding the right person will be the answer to all your problems and you'll be happy – but you *can* be happy without a partner. I'm not asking you to *pretend* to love being single, I'm saying there are many good things about being single, and it is your job to genuinely find them. You *can* do this, and it will open the door to happiness, be that with an ideal partner soon or happily single for the time being. I'm not asking you to love being single forever – just right now, this week, for example. Why ruin another week thinking you're in the wrong place in your life?

I remember a time I was single, a friend of mine (who was in a wonderful relationship) told me that there were still times she missed aspects of being single, and that I ought to start appreciating my single time while I still could. After all, she said, I might meet someone in a few days and then wish that I'd done more with my singleness, rather than constantly trying to find the love of my life. Her words struck a chord. So, although it felt strange at first, I made lists about being single and started loving it so much that I actually wondered why anyone wanted to get into a couple at all! And then, guess what, in just a few days I got into an amazing relationship, for the first time in a long time. It sounds like I got what I wanted when I didn't want it – which is sort of true. But the thing is, deep down I *did* want a relationship and this particular relationship immediately felt "right" to me. As I loved my moment just as it was, all sense of longing fell away. I was in my power, so to speak.

It may seem strange to do this – I know it did for me – but you want to get so excited about being single that you don't even know if you want to meet anyone anymore. Remember, you are not loving being single forever, but just for today or this week. You're not making a list to "make a relationship happen", you're simply doing it because it *is* great to be single – and it's your job to find out why. So, get out a pen and paper and write a *"What's Good About…" List* about being single.

Loving All Parts of Your Dating Self

When you do start dating someone, it can actually bring more fear and many people have shared with me how they worry about making mistakes, like falling in love "too quickly" or being "too keen". And guess what, they probably *will* do what they've always done, at least initially. So rather than try to change those things you usually do, just be kinder to yourself when you do them. In other words, you might still find yourself checking their social media like a detective. Or sending "too many" texts. You want to love yourself anyway. When you do this – which means you love yourself unconditionally and are kinder and more understanding with yourself – you will find that those unwanted behaviours will drop, all by themselves.

People tend to mirror your own self-opinion – so don't be surprised when other people agree that you are "too clingy" or "insecure" if that's what you've been telling yourself. Other people are just agreeing with *our* opinion; they are simply telling us what we tell ourselves. It works the other way, too: when you love your quirks (such as "over texting") you will be less "desperate, crazy person" and more "isn't it amazing that she cares so much about me and sends me all these great messages".

Using a "*What's Good About* my mistakes" list, go through those other "mistakes" you often make when dating – and find a way to embrace them. After all, you're in the habit of doing them anyway; this is you at the moment. And not wanting to do them isn't helping, in fact, it just makes you extra annoyed with yourself when you do them… "again". It never works to feel ashamed of yourself – instead, you want to embrace *all* of you, the parts you like and the parts you want to change. The key is, love all parts of yourself. And if you do feel ashamed, you want to embrace that, too, through practices like the *"What's Good About…" List* (see page 61) or the *Freedom Process* (see page 68).

Going for the "Wrong" Kind of Person?

People get into the whole subject of being attracted to the "wrong" type of person: they're attracted to "unavailable people" or "people who can't commit"; they criticise themselves for going for "bad boys" rather than "nice guys"; and they even do workshops in an attempt to change – but it rarely stops them being attracted to these types. Plus, now they feel like such a loser for doing it "when they should know better". *Knowing* your negative habits and *changing* them are two totally different things. Thinking your type is "wrong" is just another way to feel like *you're* wrong – and is not a good foundation to begin with: it's just more self-criticism. Instead, the place to start, as it usually is, is unconditional self-acceptance.

Being aware of your negative habits and changing them are two entirely different things. Unconditional acceptance opens the door to the already-present change you are looking for.

What if you instead chose to see that you are attracted to the *right* type of person for you right now? This is a different, and more self-affirming, way to look at it. So, let's start with knowing that nothing has gone wrong –

you are where you're meant to be and how you are is OK. Just accept yourself as you are, right now.

When you think you are into people because "they are unavailable", this just piles on the shame. It makes you think that there's something really wrong with you. It's like calling yourself "self-destructive" or one of those other unhelpful down-on-yourself labels which seem to help but don't. It's just more self-criticism to send you in the opposite direction of self-love and therefore all the answers you are looking for. And it's not accurate anyway.

In truth, you are into who you are into for many reasons – many of them well-intentioned. Perhaps your attraction was because you found him exciting, attractive and sexy with a good sense of humour? This moves you from feeling like there's something wrong with you to being able to accept yourself. When you focus on the areas of your "type" that it makes perfect sense to like, you will move into a healthier attitude and your relationships will mirror that. Trying to not be attracted to the wrong ones often just makes them *more* attractive not less, and then you're even more frustrated with yourself. I remember working with someone who decided to unconditionally love all parts of herself, and she finally dropped the shame around "her type". She got comfortable in who she was and who she had been attracted to – and now finds herself attracted to (and attracting) people who are both exciting *and* treat her respectfully.

The irony is by unconditionally accepting being into those "wrong" type of partners you end up being into the "right" ones.

Use the *"What's Good About..." List* (see page 61) to deal with any feeling or situation that you try to avoid while dating, whether it's jealousy, flirting, trust, etc. As you accept yourself, you are more likely to attract the right person and be more discerning about your feelings.

Go with the Flow of Your Feelings

Longing evolves us – but we can't long and love ourselves (or anyone else for that matter) at the same time. It can be tiring to fight what's going on. Or "hope" that he'll call. And it can also be tiring to beat yourself up for hoping that he calls, telling yourself "how desperate is that?!" It is OK to feel how you feel. It is more than OK – you are meant to feel this way right now.

So you want to embrace however you are feeling exactly as it is, and go with the current of the feeling. Of course, you wouldn't really consciously choose to feel rejected, but if you *are* feeling rejected the way out is to go with it. Go with the flow of feeling rejected. It is loving to yourself to feel rejected, if that's what you are feeling.

Repeat variations of "I should be feeling this because I am". For example, "We shouldn't be speaking right now because we're not". This may then bring up feelings of disappointment about not speaking, so you say aloud (or aloud in your mind): "I should be feeling disappointed because I am". Then you pause again and go with the next feeling that comes up, or situation that comes to your mind, and repeat "This should be happening because it is" or "I should be feeling this because I am". Don't waste this opportunity. This is a workout and a breakthrough moment. You are going to strongly resist doing this – but keep on going until you feel relief. Then move on to something else.

What you want to do is: love yourself more.

Bracing yourself to avoid these intense emotions is worse than the intense emotions themselves. And so, you want to let go into the fear, or whatever the mood currently is, by using the *Rapids Float* process (see page 50). Grab a pillow and let the mood take you. *Welcome in* not being called back, being lied to, *welcome it all.* Grab the pillow and relax into the rapids of the feeling. I know this is strange and it feels like it will take you in the wrong direction, but there is huge power in being OK with how you are feeling. When you're at home, and you have a moment, grab the "float" and relax into the rapids.

Relationship Maintenance

If you are in a relationship, the best way to keep it fresh is to spend time in appreciation. We tend to look for faults in our partners and then try to correct them. Instead, try to ignore your partner's faults and make a list of the things that are going well and the things that you love about them and the relationship.

Communication is important, so always tune into your Real Self through the practices in this book, or similar. When you put your focus more on looking for the good in your partner, you will still say what needs to be said, but you will do it more effectively. You will be heard, and changes will happen, rather than endless "over-talking" that doesn't get heard.

If you want your partner to do more to make you feel loved, that's a sign that you need to give *yourself* more love – and to love *them* more. This is the only real power you have anyway. Waiting around for your partner to change is a waste of time – it's like waiting for the mirror to change. When you change, so will your world and everything in it. This doesn't mean you put up with anything – and by all means, ask for what you need – but at the same time, work on giving yourself what you're looking to get from them.

You also want to live up to your own standards, meaning you are honest about who you are and what kind of relationship you want. Speak out who you are and what you want, so there's no room for confusion or second-guessing. This will give you great power as you are being who you say you are without the powerlessness and overthinking that being forced to lie brings. Be proudly you. Don't let someone "force you" into lying. What I mean by this is that we are happiest when we dare to be our real, authentic selves rather than holding back "because of what they might think". Be powerfully You. As I said, do this for your sake, not your partner's. The by-product is that it will benefit your partner greatly.

Freedom in Relationships

Many people wrestle with dealing with a sense of freedom and a sense of security. We want both. It seems like when we're in a relationship, we sacrifice some adventure and variety. And in a single lifestyle, it seems like we don't have the same level of security or companionship that a relationship brings. Luckily, you don't have to choose between freedom and excitement – and your partner.

The first thing to do is realize this is human – and there's nothing wrong with having this dilemma and seemingly opposing wants. Just love yourself anyway, as you are. You begin by making peace with that wanting both. Do the *"What's Good About..." List* (see page 61) on all the sides of you. Love all those aspects of you unconditionally and then, and only then, will you be able to love your partner unconditionally. What I've found, even though it's hard to believe, is you will move into a mindset where you have freedom *and* security. You and your partner will have new ideas, create new plans, more fun will come into your life, and there will be nothing lacking.

We also sometimes "go off" the relationship because we've gone off something about our own lives and are projecting feelings of emptiness on to the relationship. But boredom is due to our own overthinking and has little to do with the other person. Were you ever bored before this relationship? Of course you were – which shows it's not the relationship. You are bored with your own thoughts – and you're projecting this boredom on to your partner. The dilemma is you are not being you. Leave the relationship – and you will most likely take your mood with you. In other words, it is *your* job to create excitement in your life. And then this excitement will filter into all your relationships.

It's the same with so many emotions – like feeling trapped or confined "because of the relationship". Or feeling irritated "because of the relationship". You are trapped, confined or irritated or whatever by your own thoughts about the relationship. Or there's something else going on getting you to overthink. In many cases, it's your overthinking that's the problem. Many people sabotage their relationships by projecting in this way. If you have lost the spark, do a *Gratitude 150* (see page 72) on all the times you had the spark. Dwell on this instead. Sometimes, wanting adventure – as in with other partners – is about trying to relieve boredom not just on the subject of sex, but in general. Perhaps it is time to get a new hobby or interest?

It may be that you feel a bit obsessed with your partner and feel overly jealous or possessive. You might be more interested in *their* life than your own. If so, you need to "get a life". This could be a nudge to get more interested in your own life. Rather than abandon yourself, remind yourself that *you* are the star of your show, not them.

When you're not with your partner, crowd out all fears and doubt with lists of appreciation of him/her. List their good points, and the times they've shown you love.

Replace your overthinking with *loving them instead.* Look for all the things they are doing right. Loving them is not being a doormat – it's a gift to yourself and a key to *your* empowerment.

Hit the Pause Button

When people have asked me that question – whether to stay in their relationship or walk away – I rarely answer immediately. I know that asking this question tells me they may not be ready to make that decision and need to pause. It's clearing their overthinking (through techniques like the ones you've read in this book) that I suggest, so that they can find clarity and know just what to do.

But if you want an answer, providing there's no danger or abuse going on, my answer is more often than not: "Right now stay – *and do a process.*" Stay and clear your mind, so you *know* what to do, and you won't need to ask the question of what to do. Staying isn't about any big decisions or actions – it just means you don't leave just yet: you pause.

In this pause, I recommend getting out a pen and paper and falling back in love with your partner (through remembering the good times on a *Gratitude 150* list, see page 72) – which will help open the door to answers. I also recommend spending time in meditation to listen for guidance. Remember, it's these practices of love and silence which are key to accessing the clarity of the Real Self.

You keep on loving until your power comes back and the resolution happens. In doing so, you will love the right one in and the "wrong" one out of your life, or transform a problematic relationship for the better, if it's "meant to be". So, if in doubt – stay and love. Then you will receive certainty – a clear answer – and you will know what to do.

In that way, you will walk away in your power with only good in front of you and with no second-guessing. You see, when you leave "too soon" in a forced way, often encouraged by well-meaning friends, you open the door to regrets. Of course, you can make peace with them later, so it's no big deal – but if you can, stay and do a process first. The same goes for a job you don't like or anything. Unless it's something you can't line up with so you *have* to leave – I'd say stay as best you can. If you do leave, love yourself. We are all human, and we all have limits. From this state of being gentle with yourself, everything will be sorted in a beneficial way for everyone, and there will be no awkwardness.

CHAPTER 4
BETTER RELATIONSHIPS WITH LOVED ONES AND COLLEAGUES

Finding *your* way is the best first thing you can do to help other people find theirs.

It's difficult when you worry about your loved ones, as you can feel powerless to help them and their unhappiness can affect you. When there's someone you care about – be it your spouse or partner, parents, brothers, sisters or your kids – sometimes it's a challenge to help them feel better. You can offer support, but it can be draining when they're not listening. For them, they feel criticized. After all, no one likes being worried about. And then there's those relatives that seem to push all your buttons. Or work colleagues that really annoy or irritate you. In this section you will find practical ways to make those important relationships go better.

The Best Way to Help Others

Often we feel responsible for those we care about and feel it's our responsibility to cheer them up or save the day. But sometimes the more you try to cheer them up, the more they stay stuck, and you begin to feel worse yourself until there's a dark cloud over the both of you. What everyone really wants is that connection with their own Real Self – and forcing it rarely works. So, you're worried, which is a workout for what you want. But now it's time for the next part – to just hand it all over to life. It's reassuring how, after a period of worry – when *we* let go and step aside – that *they* find solutions, seemingly all on their own. We can keep on helping them in terms of tasks, but we don't need to get so involved with our "fixing" thoughts.

It can be frustrating when someone you are trying to help doesn't take your advice. This is where the *"What's Good About..." List* comes in (see page 61). First be OK with your own frustration or exasperation: it's understandable. For example, "She shouldn't be following my advice because she isn't" – and then list the reasons. You might write, for example:

- *Maybe it's the wrong time for her to follow it?*
- *Maybe there's a better way for her?*
- *She is finding her own power.*
- *Perhaps it's showing me where I need to follow some advice – maybe my own?*

It's OK to worry. It shows that you care. In fact, it's more than OK – worrying about someone creates a prayer for them; it evolves the very solution you are worrying about for the better. Do the *Freedom Process* (see page 68) on your worries, and you will discover this for yourself.

Higher Power List Revisited

So first, pause and make a *Higher Power List* (see page 36). When you've got some physical space from your worries and concerns, in a different room perhaps while the person in question is off doing their own thing, take out the list. On the right-hand side write, for example:

- *Sort out my relationship with Andre.*
- *Help Andre connect with his Real Self.*
- *Help Andre get a shift in his understanding so that he can feel great.*

Just throw out all those concerns you have, and write them in the form of a request, on the right-hand side.

This isn't about turning away from the person you are helping. It's about turning away from your thoughts, which are getting in the way of effective helping. Keep doing what you're doing to help, checking in on them etc. But at the same time, deal with your overthinking with these practices. For example:

"Connect _________ with His/Her Real Self"

Everyone wants this connection, and so it's not controlling to ask for this on behalf of the person you are worrying about. Drop this request on the right and get on with the left-hand side, noting down your favourite processes from the course to connect *you* such as *Focal-point Meditation* (see page 40), *"What's Good About..." List* (see page 61), etc. At first, it was their problem, but now their influence has made *you* disconnect. And so, the best thing we can now do is connect, while continuing to offload any worries about them on the right-hand side as they come up.

You may think the answer is to keep sharing the ideas in this book with the person in question and trying to get *them* to do the techniques in it, but they may not be listening. Doing *your* practices is usually the first place to start. Sometimes when there are people around you "not helping themselves", it's a nudge for *you* to practise what you know, rather than telling others to do it. First, help yourself.

Ask yourself: "Am I meditating regularly, as much as I said I would?" Then, focus on you.

When you do your own practices, your power of influence will be a lot more powerful and authentic, and you will inspire people as you are doing what you know rather than just talking about it.

"Surround ____ with Angels, Bringing Him/Her into Perfect Balance, Healing and Happiness"

If you find yourself in worry about a situation or a person, perhaps a friend or family member is going through something and you have concerns, surround the person or situation with angels, writing this request or prayer on the right-hand side of the list. In your mind's eye, fill their home with angels, light and love. You may want to visualize these angels in the form that you know will appeal to them – these loving guiding beings of light. Or you might want to see them surrounded by spiritual figures you know that they relate to, from their own spiritual path, for example. Or some other appealing figure – whatever is a representation to you or to them of that beautiful and powerful divine energy. This allows *you* to relax, knowing it is done. You don't have to think about it – you don't have to take it all on – you can let the "angels" deal with it, or whatever word you call that greater power. You can relax into this Divine Love, knowing the best support there is, is right here, now.

Dealing with Anger

If you have become angry or irritated with someone you love, realize that you are human and that this is OK. No one is perfect all of the time.

Shaming ourselves for being angry doesn't make the anger go away, it represses it and makes it worse.

We are sometimes shamed for our anger. No one particularly likes you getting irritated with them – so don't look to them for approval. In fact, some people project their own anger on to others by saying it's other people who are angry, not them, and *they* need to deal with it. Such is the shame about anger, few people own it. Not owning it, not accepting it just as it is, leads to repression and acting out of this anger.

So, once you've got angry and expressed it with angry words and a raised voice, for example – what can you do? All you can do right now is to be OK with what's happened and look for the good in it. For example, anger may have caused you to evolve into a better place. You can even do a *"What's Good About..." List* for anger (see also page 61). For example:

- *Expressing my anger made me feel a little better.*
- *Everyone gets angry sometimes.*
- *Even babies, who are so adorable, get angry sometimes, but they feel no guilt and swiftly move on from it.*

And so it is OK to lose your temper. That's how we learn. Love yourself. As you love yourself, this will also get you to understand other people's outbursts. When you first give *yourself* the benefit of the doubt, you can more easily give *them* the benefit of the doubt.

You will find that as you accept yourself, even in your anger – and then, in turn, you accept others in *their* anger – you become less angry, less of the time. This is another example of how the mind works, and how once you stop the battle with where you are right now, things change for the better. By embracing where you are, you are free to feel good. Because the Real Self doesn't know anger, when we embrace ourselves into that Real Self, the clouds of anger simply go.

> As you love yourself – all parts of you – you become your Real Self which does not know of anger.

Ultimately, though, anger keeps your lower-self mind in control. It's a vicious cycle of getting irritated, and then angry, then guilty, then irritated, and angry. When you react or talk from this mood, it just creates more problems. There's huge momentum to want to "talk it out" when you are in this state.

Talking it out when angry – or in any overthinking state when you feel less than who you are – means you are "speaking snowstorm". When you are in the snowstorm of overthinking, you probably have the urge to start speaking. But what you will say will be in snowstorm language – pointless, misunderstood and likely to have a negative impact. So, pause. Be aware that if you don't pause, you will speak snowstorm. Instead, let the thoughts settle. (Of course, be OK with yourself if you do speak snowstorm – we all do sometimes and it's all good – it's evolving the more productive aspects of our speech even more.) Often people say "Oh, I can't help my temper" – and yet in certain situations like at a job interview or around a workplace or an important meeting they hold it in quite easily. And so, you *can* help it, it just takes practice. And holding it is a gift to yourself. It's all about counting to ten before you speak. Settling in, connecting with your Real Self and *then* speaking.

If you are having a problem with a work colleague or a family member, and they are making you feel angry or any other unwanted emotion, again use the *Higher Power List* (see page 36). Write, for example, "Show me the best in [*add their name*]." And then move to a list of gratitude about family members and work colleagues. Write the various people's names at the top of the page – one page for each person, perhaps – and then list as many good things as you can find about them. It doesn't have to be 150 things like I mentioned in the course – but write as many as you can.

Relationships with Parents

People think the job of their parents is to unconditionally accept and support them just as they are, but this experience is rare, and so we need to realize how much pain this expectation can cause. Of course, it would be nice if your parents (and everyone else, for that matter) did offer unconditional acceptance and support, but that is not their job – it's your job. Parents, along with everyone else, are there to mirror you, so that *you* can find your empowerment. What I've found is our parent's predominant job once we are grown up can be to push our buttons, which means to mirror back our weak points and then tell us this information. And they're often very good at that!

Most of the people I've worked with who have a bad emotional relationship with their parents have misunderstood their parents' function. They might be furious and hurt that they are not being championed – and they cannot take being criticized. What they don't realize is their parents' lack of support is often their own criticism being mirrored back at them. It's a gift – like working with a number one gym trainer. Because we *want* to see our self-criticism in full view so we can change it.

Everyone deals with self-criticism, so I'm not saying if you have critical parents you are more self-critical than those who don't. I'm just giving you a way to use this "negativity" to your advantage. Whether your parents are around or not, this practice is useful – as we can carry the parent/child relationship in our minds.

First do a *Higher Power List* (see page 36): "Sort out my relationship with my parents". Now you can get on with your "left-hand side" work – which may include, for example, the *Magic Button* (see page 88).

Looking back at the *Magic Button*, let's use the example of "My parents believe in me, and unconditionally accept and approve of me." Write this (or a similar example of where you need approval from someone – it doesn't have to be your parents) at the top of the page. And below this sentence, you are going to write how you think you'd feel if your parents *did* approve of you. For example:

If I could press a button: "My parents believe in me and accept my career choice/lifestyle."

- *I want to feel respected.*
- *I want to feel approval for myself.*
- *I want to feel championed.*
- *I want to feel good enough.*
- *I want to feel acknowledged and believed in.*
- *I want to feel self-belief.*
- *I want to feel free.*
- *I want to feel empowered.*
- *I want to feel that I am doing the right thing.*

So I want to ask you – which would you choose, if you had the choice: your parents agreeing with your lifestyle choices or *you* approving of yourself? And can you be sure if they did approve of your lifestyle, that it would be enough to make you consistently feel good? After all, many people get the approval of their parents and still don't feel good enough. Can you say if your parents believed in you, then you would consistently believe in yourself?

Would you rather the first thing happen, that your parents believe in you and accept your career choice/lifestyle (or whatever you have written there), or would you want the list of "I want to feel…" to happen, in other words, to believe in yourself? Which would you choose if you could only choose one?

So, you'd choose the latter, to fully *know* that list of "I want to feel…" for yourself. Now you know what it really is that you want – you can thank your parents for not approving of your lifestyle. What's been happening is just a mirror to show you where *you* don't approve of you. Your parents are gifts, mirroring what you feel about yourself in this area. When you understand this and start working toward feeling these "I want to feel" statements – which means you feel more confident – your parents will shift to approve of you, or you'll be OK with them anyway even if they don't; it won't bother you, in other words. And if it does bother you – you've got a muscle to train.

Using the *Magic Button* on Other Relationships

You can also use *Magic Button* when you feel you need resolution. Sometimes we just keep on obsessing about a situation, which is giving our power away. We go into all that complication of trying to figure things out and go down all the possibilities, often worrying ourselves in the process. This doesn't lead anywhere. If you're doing that, pause and ask yourself what it is that you really want. In other words – how do you want to feel?

Example – a close friend or family member is ill, and you feel powerless. If you could press a button: "This person would be in perfect health, feeling amazing and loving life."

So, write down the situation you want to happen. In this case, you want someone to be well again – something you may not be able to control right now. And underneath this, you write the feelings you think that you'll have if this were to happen. Write "I want to feel" in front of each feeling description. For example:

- *I want to feel reassurance.*
- *I want to feel that everything is going to be OK.*
- *I want to feel safe.*
- *I want to feel blessed.*
- *I want to feel loved by life.*
- *I want to feel confident.*
- *I want to feel secure and trust in life.*

Feeling out of control is difficult – and this technique sorts that out. When you "press the button" you call your power back. And then life reflects this new feeling of confidence that you have got without the situation having to have first changed the way you wanted it to. When people get the feeling first, it's amazing how situations "out there" change to match it.

This is a difficult question – but right now do you want the situation to sort out instantly OR do you want to consistently feel the feelings you've listed, which means you could confidently deal with whatever happens?

Another example – you've been picked on or bullied. If you could press a button: *"The situation sorts itself out, and all people involved 'wake up', are dealt with and learn their lesson."*

- *I want to feel calm.*
- *I want to feel relaxed.*
- *I want to feel empowered.*
- *I want to feel validated.*
- *I want to feel heard and acknowledged.*
- *I want to feel safe.*
- *I want to feel powerful.*

- *I want to feel strong.*
- *I want to feel loved and protected.*

Would you rather the situation sorts itself out – and all people involved "wake up", are dealt with justice and learn their lesson? Or would you rather feel how you want to feel, all the time? Which would you choose if you could only choose one? Can you see that the reason you want this situation to happen is that you think it would make you feel all those feelings you wrote about?

The thing is when we give *ourselves* what we needed from the person or the situation – feeling calm, relaxed and empowered first – often what we wanted to happen happens anyway. And so, we get both things happening – what we wanted *and* our feelings of confidence. The technique itself is enough to wake you up and realize it's about giving yourself what you are looking "out there" to get.

CHAPTER 5

FORGIVENESS, LETTING GO AND DEALING WITH JUDGEMENT

Live your life and be free.

Some people get confused and think forgiveness means somehow being a doormat. But it is not. Forgiveness means "forgoing" those uncomfortable thoughts within you – getting rid of them in other words – and dropping into your Real Self. Forgiveness is seeing clearly; it's revealing the truth in the situation. It's got little to do with the other person – you don't have to speak to them again if you don't want to – it's more about letting go of the uncomfortable details and making space for wonderful new people and experiences in your life.

You may feel like the total good guy in a situation, but still, you don't feel free. It's like there's an underlying uneasiness. Forgiveness is needed. You've been reading about how to forgive. You've been trying to forgive, but you've been doing that for years, and you're still not free – it's not happening.

Forgiving doesn't mean the other person was right – that something that isn't OK is now OK. This conventional explanation of forgiveness puts you in an impossible position: it says that you somehow have to be alright with what you're not alright with – to put your own feeling of being hurt aside and say to someone "it's OK what you did" while gritting your teeth and not believing a word of it. So, you try, and fail, and feel even worse. You haven't forgiven, and you feel bad that you haven't. But this is an old and outmoded view of forgiveness that isn't working well for anyone, it's not just you.

Instant Forgiveness

A man I was coaching told me of a powerful experience with the *Higher Power List* (see page 36) and forgiveness. He wrote, "Sort out this relationship with Sam and me." (He hadn't seen Sam for years – though the relationship was still playing out in his mind almost daily.)

He explained: "Sam had slept with someone else and not admitted it, which created havoc in our relationship. There were a lot of lies, and I couldn't seem to move on. That night, after doing just this one *Higher Power List,* I had a dream in which I saw the situation entirely differently – and all was forgiven in an instant. I could have never made this dream happen myself, and I had spent hours reading hundreds of relationship articles online searching for how to forgive – it was exhausting, and it hadn't worked. But here, in an instant, the moment that I surrendered, I met with the answer. I don't feel it's a coincidence that I had surrendered the situation on my list the night before. From that point, I stopped thinking about Sam and have since moved on into an incredible relationship, which I believe was being "held up" by all the obsessing about Sam."

Use the following steps to find forgiveness:

1. Hand it all over by writing, for example, "Give me a new perspective" on the *Higher Power List.* Other statements you can write on the right-hand side are: "Sort out this situation with fairness and justice" and also "Help me keep on loving no matter what" and "Show me the truth in this situation".
2. Forgive yourself through accepting your feelings: The place to start is with you. Your mind chatter loves pointing "out there" at other people or situations to distract from and get

the focus off where real change happens – which is you. Another trick of the lower-self mind is trying to get us to love them before we've loved us – which doesn't work. So first use the *"What's Good About…" List* (see page 61)and the *Freedom Process* (see page 68) to be OK with your anger, upset, your feeling bullied, scared, defensive etc. Remind yourself that it's OK to feel how you do and you're just going to stay with yourself through it. To create the gains, all these stormy feelings are valid – everything is – and you can't go wrong. These feelings are OK, and it's your job to know this for yourself and accept yourself. Your feelings of unforgiveness are also necessary for evolving love in yourself and the situation. And now you want to do the final stage of letting go – you want to look for the good in *them*.

3. Look for the good in them, and the situation itself. This third step is the most radical step of all – an invitation to look for the good in the person you are not forgiving, through a gratitude list (see page 72). Remember things like a good sense of humour, or that they are well-dressed or evidence where you've seen them show kindness. You can even look for the benefits their action brought you (even if it is just that it's teaching you unconditional love, which will benefit all parts of your life). Get so into appreciating there's no room for analysis and overthinking and judging or anything that isn't of your Real Self. This will give *you* power. When you look for the good in them – your "enemy" – you literally love them out of your mind. Remind yourself you are doing it for you. In this way, love is a weapon. And it's the only weapon that works anyway (all the others have a side pointing at you and boomerang back), and it will open the way for justice, without you having to get involved. Love won't make you a doormat. And it's not about rewarding them – loving *them* sets *you* free.

Love is the only "weapon" that works – and your key to victory.

You can't be afraid of someone – and appreciate them at the same time. You've just got to love them. *You love them out of the way.* Love them out of your mind so you can love yourself fully. It has to be real, and that is why you want to find those things you authentically like, put pen to paper. You can't fake it by pretending to like someone you really don't like. Love opens the door to the gains. You get your power back by loving them. Loving them doesn't mean you give up your values or you become weak. It means you send love rather than attack. And that means love comes back to you many times over. That's all it means – it's not about action or even words or talking to them (you might never speak to them again, and that's OK). It's about your relationship with you; it's about sending love. It's about using the situation to get into your Real Self.

The mind chatter "bans" us from liking those people who "don't deserve it" – but that's not advantageous for us.

What will help you love them is seeing the person you have a problem with as a two-year-old child – which inside, they still are. In your mind's eye, imagine them as a two-year-old doing the same thing they did. It is easier to love them this way. After all, you'd be able to overlook what a two-year-old did almost always.

Sometimes you can feel troubled by thoughts that the other person is still as they are – unchanged and not pleasant. I suggest you gently meet these thoughts with the line "Please allow him/her to learn" whenever the person comes to mind. This is a relaxing statement that gets them out of your mind, reassuring you that they will learn the lessons they need to become a more loving person. Use this phrase, which echoes the *Thought Neutralizer* (see page 56), to face the thought or image of the person when you need to.

One Question to Shift Your Perspective

Sometimes we get so fixated in our unforgiveness that we forget about ourselves and the bigger picture. We can get so insular – the world out there seems not to exist. And so instead you want to ask, "What is the world I want?" This simple question works like magic, as it somehow manages to immediately turn your attention outward to the entire world and broadens your perspective. Don't think about answers to the question – just say the question, as many times as you want, like a mantra. It makes you ask what you would like the world to be – and broadens your horizons. It creates space in your mind to allow in new ideas. This question will defocus your viewpoint from inside to outside, in an instant, whenever you are in an obsessive mood.

Guided Journey – Forgiveness Circle

This is a popular guided journey that I have presented in my workshops and recorded for people on my coaching series, this time on the subject of forgiveness.

1. Get yourself comfortable, sit or lie down, without any other distractions around.
2. Visualize being led by an angel or guide holding your hand toward a large tent. The fabric door is opened for you and you are led into a circle and to a chair, where you take a seat.
3. You are in a huge tent, campfire in the middle with an opening at the top of the tent. Around you in the circle are wise ones, guides, guardians, some you recognize, some you don't, but you trust in them and feel their love and wisdom.
4. Opposite you there is an empty chair. You see someone else being led through a door on the other side of the tent. You recognize them as the person you have a connection with, who you need to do this forgiveness exercise with. They are seated opposite you and they look surprised when they see you opposite them.
5. There are "adjudicators" and wise ones, angels all around, who whisper to this person and offer them deep counsel. You don't have to pass judgement. You don't have to do anything. Hand over your judgement to the adjudicators;

they will speak to the other person. They will deal with the situation with fairness. The wise ones do not take sides, they surround you both with love and offer to educate both of you, show you new perspectives and open both your hearts to love.

6. Sit for a while, knowing that everything is being sorted out with justice. The other person is led away – and you feel relaxed. You are bathed in love, and they are bathed in love after the situation is sorted in a fair way.
7. When you are ready, open your eyes.

And you can make this journey whenever you feel guided – where you relax, step aside and let life sort out the situation.

Live Your Life (and Allow Others to Live Theirs)

Being judgemental, according to the dictionary, is "having or displaying an overly critical point of view." Having prejudice is described as an "unreasonable preconceived opinion that is not based on enough information". This could define many of the opinions people have about everything. We rarely have enough information to give an accurate opinion about someone else's life or even the circle of life itself. But still people try, filling newspapers and magazines and social media and chit-chat conversations up with this snowstorm of nonsense. Yes, judgements evolve us like everything does – but it's still just meaningless mind chatter passing the time and accomplishing little. Judgemental opinions are about having an opinion before you're qualified to have an opinion – about forming a viewpoint before you've seen the full picture. These viewpoints can only be false and don't get you anywhere. And sometimes, if not often, they harm others.

Diversity is a huge benefit for us all, and fearful reactions of difference are just a reflection of the lowest aspect of us – our mind chatter. When the lower-self mind sees something new, it can go into fearful overthinking. And so often-times judgement is based on fear of the unknown. That phrase says a lot, "fear of the unknown" – the subject is unknown, meaning this would be a good time to listen within and learn, keeping quiet until accurate information is received. To find soothing, first pause. Silence is a very good way of dealing with your own judgements – because in this space you realize that you don't know what you're talking about and it's time to learn: to learn to unconditionally love.

We all have preconceived judgements, so this isn't a criticism. It's just a note to all of us of the importance of rising above all of this because judgement is an obstacle to being in our Real Self; it's unpleasant not only for the one who is on the receiving end, but also the one who is judging. Being prejudiced is not natural; it's not who we are.

Releasing Judgements

Being OK with where you are right now and giving yourself the benefit of the doubt is the first step to make changes. Some people may have been brought up in a certain judgemental background, be it family, or a different era and culture – so I don't want to blame people for beginning with whatever outlook they began with. Unconditional self-love is the way to make changes, and we all start from different places.

> Unconditional acceptance releases what you don't want.

This may seem to be a condoning of bogus beliefs – but it's counterintuitive in this way. When we demand that other people change their views "or else", it's not very successful – no one likes to be forced. Whereas in the atmosphere of love, judgement fades away and right perspective arises – which isn't an opinion but unconditional love.

Judgemental people are usually equally harsh with themselves. Although they attract judgement, it's love that they need.

Deep down, we all unconditionally love everyone. So, meeting unloving views with unconditional love is the way to make them disappear like clouds on a sunny day. And what will be left is judgement's opposite: unconditional acceptance. Like the *Freedom Process* shows, closed-mindedness, for example, can be the "weightlift" for open-mindedness. The natural, real, authentic Self has no prejudice. In your Real Self, you love and accept everybody, no matter what.

Judgemental Views Against You

It's common for people with something different about them to be made to feel "less than" – and if this applies to you, you want to focus on being extra kind and gentle with yourself. Being a minority can sometimes feel like having to deal with constant rejection and can be harsh.

The thing is if someone is judging you for being different to the status quo, there's a weird kind of a compliment in this, even if you don't feel it at the time. That's because some of the most powerful and amazing people have experienced being judged – it's often envy. In fact, a lot of bullying is envy: people wishing they could be like you. The unfortunate consequence is that it trains the person who has been bullied to feel there's something wrong with them. Rather than trusting their own Self, they begin to trust the mind chatter of outside voices. They give up their power. Many of us have done this. But now you know you can find your way home to your Real Self. Plus, this time of feeling "less than" is not wasted as it can be an important phase to strengthen you, bringing with it essential gains which will benefit you – though it's very hard to see that at the time.

When I work with people who have experienced prejudice, I always recommend the *Self-realization Process* (see page 82). This is because people who have been prejudiced against often turn this outer attack or harshness against themselves – and are in such a habit of doing it that it feels normal to them. Using a mirror to connect with our eyes and reassure ourselves that we are good enough and we are loved, can turn this habit around.

We also want to take time to look for the good in our differences. So often people tell me that those unique parts of themselves they once saw as different and even an obstacle, they now realize are not only great – but an actual advantage which they wouldn't change for anything.

As you now know, our resistance against life (which includes self-criticism) is OK, as it evolves us. In other words, when you can move from disliking something about you, to loving it, your self-love will be steadfast, and you will get the "gains" from all that prior resistance. So, don't criticize yourself for any time wasted on self-criticism. It wasn't wasted – it was a workout. See it as a gift which will bring in a whole new level of life experience for you: an upgrade, if you will.

For example: "*What's Good About* being me (in my difference and uniqueness)."

- *It's given me a different perspective on life that has enriched my life.*
- *It's OK to feel as I feel.*
- *It's given me freedom from fixed society rules or judgements.*
- *I should be who I am because I am.*
- *It's got me to evolve self-confidence and a strong sense of who I am.*
- *Fear of what others think is one of the biggest blocks in the way of people being themselves – and this subject is freeing me from that.*

Being You, No Matter What: from Real Self to *Free Self*

Judgemental views are an opportunity to turn within, realize "what do they know", and instead find your own truth within. You want to be talked about. Let them talk. Whether someone loves you or dislikes you – it is attention. Their conversations about you just send you energy. Staying connected to your Real Self turns criticism into blessings. You want to radically look for the good in all of it, so it has no power over you. Let them do it, but you don't need to hear it or read it. Pay less attention to that spoken or written mind chatter of those who judge you, whether it's ranting on social media or anywhere else. Don't bother reading it – tune out – and instead tune into the wisdom within you, which arises in ideas rather than thoughts, from your Real Self.

And then, walk on and enjoy your life. Walk on centred in your Free Self, free of the tangle of thoughts and open to the flow of ideas, being you no matter what!

AFTERWORD

Set a date in your diary when you are going to begin the course – then do it.

Settle your mind with meditation and then fill it with gratitude and love, so much so that there is no room in your mind for anything else. This will benefit you – and everyone you interact with. And when you find yourself overthinking about something that isn't so good, know it's a workout – so even that is something to find a blessing in.

You might be tempted to just sit there daydreaming about your potential. Or another of the mind chatter's favourites – reading lots of books about practices rather than doing them. Reading intellectual books about the power of meditation, rather than meditating, for example. There are some good books out there, and you will be guided to the best ones for you. But too much thinking is what keeps your Real Self clouded. Many of us would prefer to read about the Real Self than do what it takes to experience it – reading about the Self does not get you into the Self. It's time to do the four-week course and experience it for yourself.

Procrastination

People ask me all the time how to deal with procrastination: "How can I make myself do the techniques? I know I ought to do them, but I just don't… I find myself surfing the internet or watching TV or talking or reading about philosophy." Or "Do you have a technique to deal with procrastination?"

I reply that even if I had a technique, you'd probably procrastinate and not do it anyway – but joking aside – the best technique I've found is this: Hire a coach. One of the best ways to deal with your procrastination and make real changes in your life is to work with someone one-to-one. Nearly every professional sports star or singer has a coach: someone to hold them to account. It's the same with many successful people in general. Their secret is a coach – a coach who knows what they are doing.

Not doing those things you know you ought to be doing is a problem most of us face. It's easier *not to* go to the gym. It's easier *not to* follow the course in this book. A coach encourages you to do the work necessary to create the result you want. That's one of the reasons people employ me to work with them.

If working with a coach isn't an option for you, there's something else you can do. You can partner with a friend to work through the course in this book. You can get together with this friend or a group of friends in a café, and sit and do the techniques together, and hold one another to account. This is what I did in the early days of developing the course.

For further resources and to find out more about Michael's seminars, workshops and one-to-one appointments visit
www.michaeljames.be